DIVING & SNO

TROPICAL

OF THE INDO-PACIFIC REGION

DIVING & SNORKELLING GUIDE TO
TROPICAL MARINE LIFE
OF THE INDO-PACIFIC REGION

RED SEA • MALDIVES • INDIAN OCEAN • THAILAND
MALAYSIA • SINGAPORE • INDONESIA • PHILIPPINES
AUSTRALIA • MICRONESIA • MELANESIA • POLYNESIA

MATTHIAS BERGBAUER and MANUELA KIRSCHNER

CONSULTANT: LAWSON WOOD

JOHN BEAUFOY PUBLISHING

Contents

Introduction 6

Fish 12

Reptiles and
Marine Mammals 152

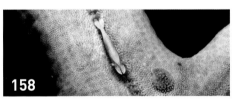

Invertebrates 158

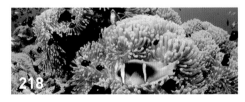

Index 218

Introduction

The abundance of different forms and species found in coral reefs gives them a biological abundance equalled only by that of the tropical rainforests, providing a home for innumerable living creatures. Despite many years of exploration, marine biologists are always discovering new species in the world's coral reefs.

One of the reasons for this diversity is the reef-building hard corals. The individual animals are very small and have a very simple structure. Each one is surrounded by a limestone skeleton and continuously deposits calcium at its basal plate, so the limestone base beneath the polyps is in a state

A garden beneath the waves: A floral wrasse (*Cheilinus chlorourus*) swims through the abundant landscape of the reef.

of constant growth. In this way they form reefs –
colonies of countless individual animals that can
be several metres across. Over many generations
and thousands of years, this constant accumulation
builds up into massive coral reefs, the largest
structures on earth created by living beings. This
is an outstanding achievement for such minute
'master builders'. During the day, hard corals
appear to be lifeless, the polyps usually being visible
only at night, when they extend their tentacles in
order to catch plankton.

Almost without exception, reef-building hard corals
have a second food source in addition to the plankton
they catch: they live in a close symbiotic relationship
with microscopic algae. These 'zooxanthellae' live
inside the cells of the polyps, where they carry out

A good location: A group
of feather stars makes
use of an exposed coral
rock to catch plankton.

Master builders: These massive coral reefs are made by minute coral polyps.

photosynthesis. Polyps and algae live as part of a nutrient exchange that benefits both partners. This mutual diet supplementation, with its highly effective recycling of nutrients, makes corals extremely productive. As a result they grow very rapidly in spite of the relatively low level of nutrients in the tropical oceans where they live.

Reef-building hard corals need very specific environmental conditions, and this limits their ability to spread. Because of their symbiotic relationship with the zooxanthellae, they require plenty of sunlight. In clear water, there is usually sufficient light for photosynthesis only up to around 50 metres. Temperature is also critical. With very few exceptions, coral reefs are able to thrive only where the average temperature of the water does not fall below 20 degrees. Another factor affecting coral growth is a high level of sediment: if the coral becomes covered with sand, it cannot survive. The sediment carried by major rivers, for example, means that coral reefs cannot live in areas influenced by estuarial flow.

In total, tropical coral reefs cover only about 0.015 per cent of the whole ocean surface, but their importance is far greater than this suggests. About one-quarter of all saltwater fish depend on coral reefs in one way or another, and almost every class of animal is represented there. This huge diversity within a small area makes coral reefs one of the most complex and fascinating environments in the world.

The Indian and Pacific Oceans, referred to jointly as the Indo-Pacific, contain around 92 per cent of the world's coral reefs. The region includes such well-known destinations as the Red Sea, the Indian Ocean with the Maldives and the Seychelles, then further east to South-east Asia with Thailand, Indonesia and the Philippines, then on to the Western Pacific with Australia and the archipelagos of Micronesia, Melanesia and Polynesia. All the species described in this book live in the Indo-Pacific.

Togetherness: Table corals shelter symbiotic algae (left); Clownfish live in symbiosis with anemones (right).

Every time we dive or snorkel in a coral reef, a wealth of species is not all that we see: we can also observe many interesting behaviour patterns. There are astonishing survival strategies that make use of camouflage and deception, tricks and ruses, but there are also a striking number of close bonds formed between different species. The various types of symbiosis are especially interesting. Among the most well known are those between anemone or clown fish and their host anemones, the ecologically vital cleaning procedures carried out by some wrasses and shrimps in partnership with hundreds of fish species, and the coexistence of many small crustaceans with a variety of reef-dwellers, such as pistol shrimps with partner gobies.

Swarms: Anthias often form large groups. They swim close to the reef to catch plankton.

Diving on a coral reef is particularly rewarding at night, providing a completely different experience from the more familiar daytime view. Most fish rest

for the night in holes and crevices, leaving the stage free for the invertebrates, who remain hidden during the day. These include numerous crustaceans, sea urchins, snails, feather stars, brittle stars, cuttlefish and squid. The changeover from day to night is almost like a change of shift in the animal world.

Finally, a coral reef is always sure to provide surprises, because it is often visited by other ocean creatures – hunting for food, visiting the cleaner stations, or simply passing through. Encounters with sea turtles, for example, are not unusual on many reefs. If you are lucky and your timing is right you might also see large fish such as eagle rays and manta rays, a range of sharks, including whale sharks, or mammals such as dolphins.

Search party: Powder-blue surgeonfish and convict fish patrol the reef in search of edible algae.

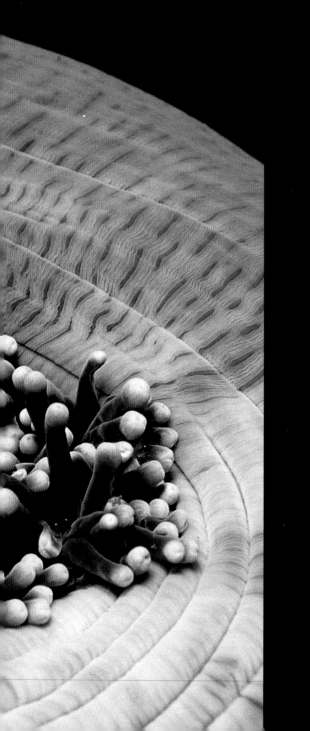

Fish

Nurse sharks
Orectolobiformes

Apart from the whale shark, all members of this group of sharks live on the seabed. They are generally harmless to humans if left undisturbed.

Whale shark: This is the largest fish of all, but despite its size and its mouth of up to 130 cm in width it feeds harmlessly on plankton. It holds its mouth wide open and moves unhurriedly along, straining large volumes of water for plankton and also catching small fish and crustaceans in the process. Whale sharks are often accompanied by other fish, including jacks, cobias and remoras.

Leopard shark: This unmistakable shark rests on the seabed during the day and goes in search of food at night, both on the reef and in nearby sandy areas. It eats molluscs and gastropods, also crustaceans and bony fish. This species is also known as the zebra shark because the juveniles are striped.

Nurse shark: Nurse sharks have barbels that contain taste sensors, and these help them to find their food. They feed at night on octopus, crustaceans, fish, sea urchins and even sea snakes. They can crush hard-shelled animals using their powerful jaws.

Whale shark
Rhincodon typus

Length: 1,200 cm
Biology: Active both day and night, not timid. Juveniles in small groups, adults mainly individually; 1–130 m.
Distribution: Circumtropical

Leopard shark
Stegostoma fasciatum

Length: max. 320 cm
Biology: Frequently on sand and gravel close to reefs. Juveniles rarely seen and thought to live below 50 m; 1–65 m.
Distribution: Red Sea to Samoa

Tawny nurse shark
Nebrius ferrugineus

Length: 320 cm
Biology: Often territorial if undisturbed. Usually rests in caves or under ledges during the day; 1–70 m.
Distribution: Red Sea to French Polynesia

Bull sharks
Carcharhinidae

Bull sharks or man-eating sharks are fast, agile swimmers. The ones illustrated here are typical reef-dwellers and are a frequent sight in many areas.

The blacktip reef shark can be encountered even in the 10-metre zone. It often hunts over the reef top, when its dorsal fin may stick out of the water. Young sharks in particular will even swim at knee depth.

The whitetip reef shark also patrols its territory during the day, but tends to be more active at night. It normally rests in the daytime – individually, in pairs or in small groups – at a regular spot, perhaps under a ledge or in a cave, but also on open sand in deeper water. These sharks can live for at least 25 years.

The grey reef shark is territorial and has an extensive homewater area. In the pecking order of the reef it is the dominant species, outranking the blacktip and whitetip reef sharks. It hunts for bony fish such as moray eels, soldier and surgeon fish, and also preys on cephalopods and large crustaceans.

Blacktip reef shark
Carcharhinus melanopterus

Length: 180 cm
Biology: Individually or in groups; timid; eats reef fish and squid; 0–75 m.
Distribution: Red Sea to French Polynesia

Whitetip reef shark
Triaenodon obesus

Length: 180 cm
Biology: Eats reef fish and squid. Will force itself into even narrow crevices in search of prey. Non-aggressive, timid; 1–330 m.
Distribution: Red Sea to Panama

Grey reef shark
Carcharhinus amblyrhynchos

Length: 180 cm
Biology: Lives in outreefs and reef channels, likes strong-current areas; sometimes exhibits threatening behaviour in the Pacific; 1–275 m.
Distribution: Red Sea to Easter Island

Rays
Batoidei

Rays are cartilaginous fish with a flattened, disc-shaped body. Most are typical bottom-dwellers and can be seen even in very shallow water on areas of sand. It is also not unusual for them to bury themselves, with only their eyes and breathing holes visible. They swim using wave-like movements of their body edges, usually staying close to the ground.

Flying aces: The devilfish, eagle rays and cownose rays are different. They have freed themselves from their bottom-dwelling habits and can swim for long periods with great elegance, 'flying' with wing-like movements of their broad triangular pectoral fins through open water over long distances. The manta ray is a plankton filter feeder and is the largest of all the rays at 1.5 tonnes.

Swordsmen: Unlike the above harmless giants, stingrays have one or more venomous stings on the top of their tails – a dangerous defensive weapon.

Manta
Manta birostris

Length: up to 670 cm across
Biology: Individually or in groups of up to 50; regularly seen on reefs, where it also visits cleaner stations; 1–50 m.
Distribution: Circumtropical

Spotted eagle ray
Aetobatus narinari

Length: 230 cm across
Biology: Individually, in pairs or in schools of up to 200; visits reefs, where it burrows in the sand for molluscs and crustaceans; 1–80 m.
Distribution: Circumtropical

Porcupine ray
Urogymnus asperrimus

Length: 100 cm across
Biology: Active both day and night; burrows for prey, including crustaceans, worms and wrasses sleeping in the sand; 1–30 m.
Distribution: Red Sea to Fiji

Black-spotted stingray
Taeniura meyeni

Length: 164 cm across
Biology: Sand and gravel reef areas; eats fish and invertebrates that live on the seabed; non-aggressive, but there have been fatal incidents where divers have tried to ride on the animals; 3–500 m.
Distribution: Red Sea to Galapagos

Kuhl's stingray
Dasyatis kuhlii

Length: 50 cm across
Biology: A common species on sand or mud surfaces, normally close to the reef. Frequently covers itself with sand, making it difficult to spot. Eats invertebrates living in the sand; 0.5–90 m
Distribution: South Africa to Samoa

Blue-spotted stingray
Taeniura lymma

Length: 35 cm across
Biology: Sand and gravel reef areas. Visits cleaner stations. Active by day and night; scrabbles in the bed for molluscs and worms; often rests during the day under ledges and table corals; 2–30 m.
Distribution: Red Sea to Fiji

Leopard torpedo
Torpedo panthera

Length: 100 cm long
Biology: Mostly on sand; not rare, but usually buried. Uses electric shocks from its pair of special organs to stun bottom-dwelling fish, including scorpionfish; 0.5–55 m.
Distribution: Red Sea and Gulf of Aden

Moray eels
Muraenidae

Moray eels look frightening, but in fact are not aggressive at all. The few accidents reported are mostly the result of feeding, threatening or harpooning the animals. Morays accustomed to being fed lose their fear and can become intrusive. The regular opening and closing of the mouth is not a threatening gesture but is for breathing purposes. When the mouth is closed, inhaled water rich in oxygen is pumped across the gills and expelled through the small gill opening at the back of the head.

A good nose: During the day they stay in holes and crevices, often peeking out a little from their hiding places. At night they prowl the reef looking for prey, relying mainly on their acute sense of smell because they have poor eyesight. Species with sharp fangs eat mainly fish, while those with tapered teeth eat crustaceans, sea urchins and snails.

Giant moray
Gymnothorax javanicus

Length: 230 cm
Biology: Eats fish, also young whitetip reef sharks; occasionally crustaceans and octopus; 1–46 m.
Distribution: Red Sea to Panama

Honeycomb moray
Gymnothorax favagineus

Length: 220 cm
Biology: Diurnal and nocturnal, not timid. As well as on reefs, it is sometimes found in open seaweed meadows; 1–50 m.
Distribution: Southern Red Sea to Samoa

Fimbriated moray
Gymnothorax fimbriatus

Length: 80 cm
Biology: Hunts at night for fish and crustaceans, so seen more often then than during the day; timid and nervous; 1–50 m.
Distribution: Seychelles, Maldives to French Polynesia

Blackcheek moray
Gymnothorax breedeni

Length: 120 cm
Biology: Lives in outreefs with strong currents; do not approach too closely – this species can be aggressive and can bite very quickly; 4–25 m.
Distribution: Comores, Seychelles, Maldives to French Polynesia

Whitemouth moray
Gymnothorax meleagris

Length: 120 cm
Biology: White mouth interior gives it a distinctive appearance; active by day and night, feeds mainly on fish and crustaceans; 0.3–36 m.
Distribution: Red Sea to Galapagos Islands

Geometric moray
Gymnothorax griseus

Length: 65 cm
Biology: Lives in rock and coral reefs;
common species, frequently seen by day
between seaweed and gravel; young often
in groups (of up to 10) in a hiding-place;
1–30 m.
Distribution: Red Sea to West Indies

Ribbon moray
Rhinomuraena quaesita

Length: 120 cm
Biology: Changes sex from male to female
as it grows: juveniles black, male (65 cm
and over) blue and yellow, female (94 cm
and over) yellow; 1–57 m.
Distribution: East Africa to French
Polynesia

Snake eels
Ophichthidae

The snake eel family consists of roughly 290 species, yet they are rarely seen by divers.

Underground: This is because most species spend their lives buried in sand or soft sediment with only their heads or eyes protruding. Divers see them most frequently at night. Often confused with sea snakes, they are in fact bony fish, their closest relatives being the moray eels. Most species have a hard, narrowly tapering tail, which they can use to dig themselves very quickly backwards into the sand or sediment. They can even move away backwards under the sand. Some types have similar colouring to sea snakes, but they are easy to tell apart: sea snakes have visible scales, whereas snake eels are smooth-skinned. They also have fin membranes and pectoral fins, which sea snakes do not.

Marbled snake eel
Callechelys marmorata

Length: 85 cm
Biology: Easily identified by its white/cream background with distinct, evenly-distributed black spots. Not a common species despite its wide distribution. Lives in sandy areas of reefs and in sand and sediment surfaces near reefs. Hunts at night for small fish and crustaceans, using its sense of smell to guide it; 3–25 m.
Distribution: Red Sea to French Polynesia

Napoleon snake eel
Ophichthys bonaparti

Length: 75 cm
Biology: Easily recognized by its attractively patterned head. The rest of its body, marked with wide dark-coloured stripes, resembles that of the sea snake. Lives in fine to coarse sand on coastal and outer reefs, and in lagoons. Occasionally seen at night in open water. An ambush predator of small fish and squid. Will bite in self-defence; 1–20 m.
Distribution: East Africa to French Polynesia

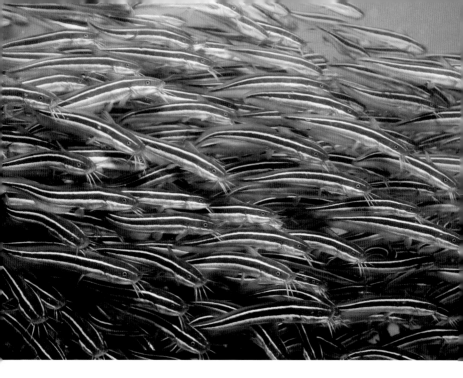

Eeltail catfish
Plotosidae

There are over 3,000 species of catfish, but most of them live in fresh water. Those that live in the sea include the striped eel catfish – the only one seen with any frequency by divers and snorkellers, depending on location. It eats bottom-dwelling species such as crustaceans and molluscs, and also fish, which it detects by means of the barbels on its mouth. During the breeding season the male sets up a nest beneath a rock, where he guards the eggs.

Striped eel catfish
Plotosus lineatus

Length: 33 cm
Biology: Lives in lagoons, coastal reefs and seaweed meadows. The juveniles form dense, spherical groups ('catfish balls') which are kept together by scent (pheromones). Adults individually or in small groups. Do not try to approach these fish: their pectoral and ventral fins have stings that can cause severe – in rare cases dangerous – poisoning; 1–60 m.
Distribution: Red Sea to Samoa

Lizardfish
Synodontidae

These small ambush predators with large mouths and numerous sharp teeth are common in most areas. Divers who approach them carefully will be allowed to come very close, but the fish will then rush away at the last moment and settle again a few metres away. Lying motionless on sand or gravel, rock or coral, they dart forward to capture tiny fish, which they swallow whole.

Two-spot lizardfish
Synodus binotatus

Length: 13 cm
Biology: Lizardfish, including this species, are able to change colour to match their background, when their spotted pattern means they are easily overlooked. Their variable colouring makes them difficult to distinguish among the various but rather similar species on the reef: in the case of this particular species, the two black dots on the tip of the nose help to identify it; 1–30 m.
Distribution: Gulf of Aden, Maldives to Hawaii and Tonga

Frogfish
Antennariidae

Despite being brightly coloured, frogfish are very well camouflaged: they blend perfectly into their surroundings, or they resemble sponges. If necessary, they are able to change colour over a period of days.

Hoaxer: On its upper lip, the frogfish has a movable fishing rod with what looks like fleshy 'bait' at the end. Any predator attracted by this apparently tasty snack will swim right in front of it's mouth.

Fast food: The frogfish can open its mouth and suck in its victim with astonishing speed: just six thousandths of a second – a world record! No other vertebrate can seize its prey so quickly.

Slow motion: The frogfish uses its pectoral and ventral fins to walk over the ground in two different ways – a step-by-step motion or a gallop, the latter being the slowest in the animal kingdom. It swims for short distances using the principle of jet propulsion, taking water into its mouth and expelling it through its nozzle-shaped gills. Its jet 'engine', too, is the slowest of any.

Giant frogfish
Antennarius commersoni

Length: 30 cm
Biology: The largest species. Very variable in colour: white, yellow, pink, red, orange, greenish, brown and black are known. The fish are frequently the same colour all over, but sometimes have flecks of other colours with a crusted appearance. Often found under ledges, and very fond of living among sponges. Individually or in pairs; 1–70 m
Distribution: Red Sea to Panama

Painted frogfish
Antennarius pictus

Length: 21 cm
Biology: A highly variable species, with local colour variants and possibly subspecies, so identification is often difficult. Its skin texture allows it to mimic sponges, including the inlet and outlet openings (see photo). Often found on sponges, also on living coral, gravel, and sand or sediment. Also eats lionfish; 1–70 m.
Distribution: Red Sea to French Polynesia

Soldierfish and squirrelfish
Holocentridae

Red Guard: The colour red dominates in most species of this family, which is divided into two sub-families, soldierfish and squirrelfish. They all also have large eyes and clearly visible scales. The most obvious differences are the squirrelfish's head that tapers to a point, and the large spike on its gill covers; soldierfish have more rounded heads and no spike, or only a very small one.

Nocturnal: These fish are active mainly at night, which is why they have large, light-sensitive eyes. However, despite their nocturnal habits they are readily seen at close quarters during the day, when they wait, moving gently, in the shelter of caves or ledges, or beneath table corals. Some species are seen individually, others in small groups, while yet others form dense shoals. They leave their refuges at night, when soldierfish hunt for zooplankton in open water. Squirrelfish feed on bottom-dwelling species such as crustaceans, worms and even small fish.

Sabre squirrelfish
Sargocentron spiniferum

Length: 45 cm
Biology: The largest species; spends the day under ledges; not timid, allows divers to come very close; 1–122 m.
Distribution: Red Sea to Hawaii and Australia

White-tip soldierfish
Myripristis vittata

Length: 20 cm
Biology: Spends the day under ledges, mostly on the slopes of outreefs, often in large, tight concentrations; 15–80 m.
Distribution: East Africa to French Polynesia

Spotfin squirrelfish
Neoniphon sammara

Length: 32 cm
Biology: Common species, not very timid. Can often be seen moving across staghorn corals and between rocks; 2–45 m.
Distribution: Red Sea to Hawaii and French Polynesia

Cornetfish
Fistulariidae

The extremely elongated cornetfish stalks small fish, taking them by surprise and grabbing them with a sudden dart forward. Its narrow, tube-shaped snout means it can catch only relatively small prey, sucking them in as with a pipette. It can change colour within seconds from silvery green to a very pale or dark greyish-brown.

Cornetfish
Fistularia commersonii

Length: 150 cm
Biology: Patrols the reef individually or in loose groups. Feeds on small fish and crustaceans. Sometimes swims 'piggyback', hidden behind a larger fish in order to approach smaller fish unnoticed; may also do the same with divers; 1–128 m.
Distribution: Red Sea to Panama

Trumpetfish
Aulostomidae

Closely related to the cornetfish, trumpetfish use the same hunting method, including the trick of swimming close to other fish so they can creep up on their prey unawares. Juveniles and adults have different colouring. Individuals are able to modify their colour pattern; in some areas there is a yellow (xanthic) colour variant.

Trumpetfish
Aulostomus chinensis

Length: 80 cm
Biology: Usually individually, sometimes also in loose pairs. Sometimes stands vertically among horn corals for camouflage. The trumpetfish family consists of only two species: in addition to the Indo-Pacific type illustrated here, there is also another species that lives in the Atlantic, including the Caribbean; 1–122 m.
Distribution: South Africa to Panama

Needlefish
Belonidae

Needlefish are very elongated predators with a pointed snout and numerous needle-like teeth. They live in surface waters, catch small fish, and are very well camouflaged with their silvery-blue colouring. To evade their enemies they are able to catapult themselves out of the water at incredible speed.

Crocodile houndfish
Tylosurus crocodilus

Length: 135 cm
Biology: Lives in coastal waters; usually swims just below the surface; is able to leap out of the water and skid across the surface using its tailfin; the largest species in its family. They sometimes jump up towards fishing lights at night, and have caused injuries to anglers and fishermen. Underwater they are placid fish.
Distribution: Circumtropical

Seamoths
Pegasidae

These small, bottom-feeding fish get their name from their wing-like pectoral fins, but they move mainly in a creeping motion across the seabed. Their armoured bodies mean they are able to move only their tails. They feed on minute invertebrates. When disturbed they spread out their pectoral fins like wings.

Little dragonfish
Eurypegasus draconis

Length: 8 cm
Biology: Lives in sheltered areas such as lagoons and quiet coves, on sand, mud and gravel, often buried. Occasionally seen in pairs during the mating season. Colouring variable and depends on their background: whitish against light-coloured sand, to dark brown against a darker background; 1–90 m.
Distribution: Red Sea to French Polynesia

Ghost pipefish
Solenostomidae

Only five species are known in this small but interesting family. They are excellently camouflaged and are thus often overlooked. Even if a diving guide points out a feather star to a group, it usually takes a while before they spot the ornate ghost pipefish he is indicating. Searching for these fish can be like looking for a needle in a haystack. Because of this secretive lifestyle, the fifth species was not discovered and described by marine biologists until 2002. Females grow larger than males, and unlike the related pipefish and seahorses, they incubate the eggs. For this purpose the ventral fins of the females form a brood pouch which can hold several hundred eggs. The eggs hatch after 10–20 days into transparent larvae. Ghost pipefish feed on tiny shrimps and ampiphods, which they suck into their long tubular mouths.

Robust ghost pipefish
Solenostomus cyanopterus

Length: 15 cm
Biology: Colouring variable: green, yellow, grey or dark brown. Resembles seaweed, and the brown varieties usually have light-coloured speckles that look like the encrusted growths on dead seaweed. They can wave to and fro like dead leaves of seaweed in the current. Usually in pairs on sand, between algae and seaweed; 0.2–20 m.
Distribution: Red Sea to Fiji

Ornate ghost pipefish
Solenostomus paradoxus

Length: 11 cm
Biology: Has numerous grotesque skin appendages; colour variable: background colour often red, yellowish or almost black with white or yellow markings. Usually lives in the shelter of feather stars, horn or black corals. Most often swims at an angle with its head downwards; often seen in pairs, occasionally also in small groups; 2–30 m.
Distribution: Red Sea to Fiji

Seahorses
Syngnathidae

Seahorses are the strangest of finned creatures as they do not resemble fish at all. Their scaleless skin is armoured by bony rings. Seahorses swim slowly, moving through the water with gentle movements of their dorsal fins. They have a long prehensile tail, which can be rolled up into a coil, and they often use it to grip on to seaweed, horn coral or other vegetation. The tail also acts as a rudder when the seahorse is swimming.

Role reversal: It is the male seahorse who is responsible for incubating the eggs. Reproduction involves a long and complex courtship ritual which can last up to three days, after which the female lays up to 150 eggs (depending on species) in the brood pouch of the male. The eggs are then fertilized in the pouch by the male, and incubated for several weeks. When the young fish finally hatch out from the eggs, the male uses strong pumping movements to push them out into the open through a small opening in the brood pouch.

Common seahorse
Hippocampus taeniopterus

Length: 15 cm
Biology: Shallow coastal reefs, also in seaweed, estuaries, harbours and brackish water. Colouring is variable: not just yellow but also dark brown to black; 2–55 m.
Distribution: India to Hawaii and French Polynesia

Pygmy seahorse
Hippocampus bargibanti

Length: 2 cm
Biology: Lives on muricella horn coral, where the tubercles on its skin look like the closed coral polyps. If it is on gorgonian coral (*M. paraplectana*) it has orange tubercles, while on red coral (*M. plectana*) it has red ones (*see photo*). Photo right: perfect camouflage! (shown life-size); 15–50 m.
Distribution: South Japan, Philippines, Indonesia, northern Australia, possibly elsewhere

Pipefish
Syngnathidae

Pipefish, with the seahorses, form a single
family. They feed on bottom-dwelling
invertebrates and zooplankton, and some
of the larger species also eat young fish,
although these have to be very small.
Pipefish have no teeth, so their prey is
sucked in through the pipette-shaped mouth
and swallowed whole.

Network pipefish
Corythoichthys flavofasciatus

Length: 15 cm
Biology: The pipefish male
incubates the eggs, which are
transferred to his underbelly
following a long courtship ritual.
In some species the eggs lie in
a protective skin fold, in others
they are in the open and readily
visible on the male's belly. The
eggs hatch after about four weeks;
1–25 m.
Distribution: Red Sea to the
Maldives

Snipefish
Centriscidae

This family contains only four species, of
which two are deep-sea fish. The other two
are a regular sight on reefs, depending on
location. Their sharp ventral keel, which is
made of bony plates, gives them the name
razorfish. They use their toothless pipette-like
mouths to suck up plankton from the water.

Coral razorfish
Aeoliscus strigatus

Length: 15 cm
Biology: Swims close to the
bottom, sometimes in schools
of up to a hundred, always
vertically and head-downwards.
The fish only swim horizontally
when fleeing from danger, and
they quickly revert to the vertical
position. They like to remain
upside-down in among bushy horn
corals or sheltered by long-spined
sea urchins; 0.5 to at least 20 m.
Distribution: Aldabra and the
Seychelles to New Caledonia

Lionfish
Pteroinae

Lionfish are conspicuous, flamboyant fish. They often proceed slowly, almost majestically, across the reef, or they float gently on the spot with minimal movement. They are not timid and will sometimes approach – even to within touching distance – a diver who remains still.

Dangerous beauty: Many of the conspicuous fin spines are poisonous. Although no deaths have been reported and the venom is not as dangerous as has sometimes been alleged, it can cause very painful poisoning, and divers can easily be injured when trying to scare away fish that have approached them. If the fish feel threatened they can suddenly sting with outspread spines, so the best action is simply to move away if the fish get too close. Lionfish use their venom for defence, not for catching prey. They eat small fish and crustaceans. A typical hunting method is to drive smaller fish into a corner, where they then use their oversized pectoral fins as fishing nets.

Common lionfish
Pterois volitans

Length: 38 cm
Biology: Often close to ledges and caves, or in wrecks. Hunts at sundown and during the night for fish, prawns and shrimps. Opens out its pectoral fins to drive its prey into a corner. Individually or in small groups; 1–60 m.
Distribution: Red Sea to Bali and Sumbawa. The very similar red lionfish (*P. volitans*) is found from the Gulf of Thailand to the Pitcairn Islands.

Spotfin lionfish
Pterois antennata

Length: 20 cm
Biology: Common species, easily recognizable by its long, free-moving pectoral fin spines, which are joined at the base by a black-spotted membrane. Usually found under ledges and in hollows. Individually or in small groups. Usually inactive during the day, hunts for shrimps and prawns during late afternoon and at night; 1–50 m.
Distribution: East Africa; Maldives to French Polynesia

Shortfin lionfish
Dendrochirus brachypterus

Length: 15 cm
Biology: Lies in wait for prey, usually at the base of freestanding coral blocks or rocks; individually or in harems with up to 10 females; 2–80 m.
Distribution: Red Sea to Samoa

Mombassa lionfish
Pterois mombasae

Length: 19 cm
Biology: Pectoral fin spines with a dark-spotted membrane. Prefers areas with soft coral and sponges on deep outreefs; 10–60 m, rarely above 20 m.
Distribution: Red Sea (rare) to Papua New Guinea

Twinspot lionfish
Dendrochirus biocellatus

Length: 10.5 cm
Biology: Eye spots on the dorsal fin. Lives in coral-rich reefs. Timid, hides during daylight hours. Hunts at night and is normally only seen at that time; 1 to at least 40 m.
Distribution: Mauritius to the Society Islands

Zebra lionfish
Dendrochirus zebra

Length: 20 cm
Biology: Sheltered coastal reefs. Eats prawns, shrimps, fish. Begins hunting about three hours before sunset. The male defends his territory and harem aggressively; 1–73 m.
Distribution: Central Red Sea to Samoa

Scorpionfish
Scorpaenidae

Scorpionfish are typical bottom-dwellers and spend most of their time on the seabed. They have a rudimentary swim bladder and are poor swimmers. They are very reluctant to swim, and do so for no more than a few metres before sinking down to the bottom again.

Quick off the mark: Despite their ponderous appearance, they can dart forwards with extraordinary speed, and belong to the fast-movers of the fish world. Ambush predators, they wait motionless and well-camouflaged for any prey that passes close by. Then, their lethargy vanishes and they suddenly shoot forward, open their large mouths in a flash, and suck in their unwary victims. Scorpionfish have poisonous fin spines, which explain their name. However, they do not use their spines to catch prey but only for their own defence. Their poison is painful for humans but not usually dangerous.

Tasselled scorpionfish
Scorpaenopsis oxycephala

Length: 36 cm
Biology: Like other species it is capable of changing its colour in seconds to match its background; 1–43 m.
Distribution: Red Sea to Great Barrier Reef

Devil scorpionfish
Scorpaenopsis diabolus

Length: 30 cm
Biology: Frequently confused with the stonefish; if disturbed, reveals the coloured inner surface of its pectoral fins; 1–70 m.
Distribution: Red Sea to Hawaii and French Polynesia

Leaf scorpionfish
Taenionatus triacanthus

Length: 12 cm
Biology: Very variable in colour; sways sideways to resemble a leaf swaying in the swell of the sea; 1–134 m.
Distribution: East Africa to Galapagos Islands

Stonefish
Synanceinae

Landmines: Take care – this is the most poisonous fish of all. Its venomous fin spines are for defence only, but the fish are not at all timid and are difficult to scare away. The danger for divers is accidentally treading on a stonefish or brushing up against one. Although their poison is rarely fatal, it is extremely painful.

Reef stonefish
Synanceia verrucosa

Length: 38 cm

Biology: Stonefish are masters of disguise, and live up to their 'stony' name. Their hunting strategy is to sit and wait. They can remain motionless in one place for days on end. When an unsuspecting fish comes within reach, the predator opens its enormous mouth with lightning speed and sucks in its victim; sometimes several fish all lie together (three fish shown in the photo); 0.3–45 m.

Distribution: Red Sea to French Polynesia

Devilfish
Choridactylinae

True to their name: Their very name spells trouble. Devilfish do indeed have highly poisonous fin spines. They live on sand or gravel, and often bury themselves right up to the eyes and wait for passing prey. They swim rarely, preferring to crawl by means of their claw-like pectoral fin rays along the ground.

Spiny devilfish
Inimicus didactylus

Length: 19 cm
Biology: When at rest, the devilfish closes its pectoral fins and folds its caudal fin towards the body. This gives it excellent camouflage and makes it difficult to see. When it is threatened it opens out the pectoral fin and raises its tail fin so that their brilliant colours act as a warning. They can shed their skins every few months; 5–40 m.
Distribution: Andaman Sea to Vanuatu

Waspfish
Tetrarogidae

Waspfish are related to scorpionfish and, like them, have poisonous fin spines. Their most striking feature is the dorsal fin, which starts on the head in front of the eyes. Most live on soft ground. There are at least 28 species, found in shallow, tropical waters in the Indo-Pacific.

Cockatoo waspfish
Ablabys taenianotus

Length: 15 cm
Biology: Colour variable, yellow to chocolate-brown; face and body are sometimes different, contrasting colours. Creeps across the ground using its pectoral fins. Lives on sheltered sand, mud and gravel areas, individually or in pairs. Rolls over sideways to disguise itself as a dead leaf.
Distribution: Andaman Sea (Thailand) to Fiji and south-east Australia

Flatheads
Platycephalidae

Flatheads are typical bottom-dwellers and have no swim bladder. During the day, many of these ambush predators burrow into the sandy seabed to camouflage themselves. To do this they lie on the ground and make lateral shaking movements with their whole body. The sand they have stirred up then settles evenly all over them.

Tentacled flathead
Papilloculiceps longiceps

Length: 100 cm
Biology: Often more or less completely covered in sand. Not very timid. Catches shrimps, prawns and fish. It can also use a 'vertical take-off' movement to catch fish swimming a couple of metres above the seabed. Its eyes have reticulated, size-adjustable eye lappets to protect them against UV radiation.
Distribution: Red Sea to Oman; a very similar species is found as far as French Polynesia

Flying gurnards
Dactylopteridae

In fact, gurnards walk rather than fly. Flying gurnards use their modified ventral fins to walk, or rather creep, across the seabed. They spread out their huge, fan-like pectoral fins if disturbed, and can then move forward a short distance and 'glide' a little way using the rigid, extended pectoral fins. They cannot, however, 'flap' their wings.

Oriental flying gurnard
Dactyloptena orientalis

Length: 38 cm
Biology: Solitary species living on sandy bottoms in lagoons and sheltered outreefs. It is an impressive sight when gliding with its outspread pectoral fins. When the fins are folded down, however, it is relatively well camouflaged, especially if part-buried. It is able to create sounds by using its swim bladder as a resonance chamber.
Distribution: Red Sea to French Polynesia

Stargazers
Uranoscopidae

These club-shaped fish have eyes that sit on top of their heads and point upwards (hence the name 'stargazer'), and a wide, horizontal mouth opening. However, what look like teeth are really skin fringes on their lips. Some species, including all *Uranoscopus* species, have a worm-shaped flap of skin, which can be extended or retracted, on their lower jaw. This acts as a lure to attract small fish, which the stargazer seizes by rapidly opening its mouth.

Whitemargin stargazer
Uranoscopus sulphureus

Length: Approx. 35 cm
Biology: Lives on sand and mud, in lagoons and sheltered outreefs. An ambush predator, it typically buries itself in the ground, often leaving only its eyes and lips exposed, and lies in wait for passing prey. To attract its prey it is able to wave a worm-shaped extension on its lower jaw.
Distribution: Red Sea to Samoa

Tilefish
Malacanthidae

These very elongated fish live close to the seabed in sandy or gravel areas near the reef. They are seen frequently, but only from a distance, as they are very timid and alert. If danger threatens they immediately escape into burrows they have made. Tilefish eat bottom-dwelling invertebrates, or take zooplankton from the current.

Flagtail tilefish
Malacanthus brevirostris

Length: 30 cm
Biology: Individually or (mainly juveniles) in groups. Very timid, difficult to approach, but in some areas it is a very common representative of this small tropical fish family. Like other tilefish it lays its eggs inside its living-burrow; the eggs are guarded by both parents; 5–61 m.
Distribution: Red Sea to Panama

Suckerfish
Echeneidae

The primary dorsal fin of these fish has been modified to form a distinctive grooved suction disc. The fish use this like a suction cup to create a vacuum, which they use to cling on to larger creatures, which then carry them along. They like to attach themselves to various shark species, rays, large bony fish and whales, and even dugongs, turtles and ships. This small family is made up of eight species.

Sharksucker
Echeneis naucrates

Length: 110 cm
Biology: Lives in open seas but comes to reefs with its respective host, as it is often found on sharks, rays, and sometimes even turtles. Feeds on small fish, sometimes also on the prey of its host, and takes parasites from the host's surface. More frequent reef visitors are juveniles without a host – they sometimes try to attach themselves to divers! 1–60 m.
Distribution: All tropical and subtropical seas

Soapfish
Grammistinae

This small sub-family of the seabass gets its name from its slimy skin. It produces a bitter-tasting poison called grammistin, which seems to protect the fish from both predators and skin parasites. Many soapfish are nocturnal and hide in caves and crevices during the day.

Sixline soapfish
Grammistes sexlineatus

Length: 27 cm
Biology: Lives on reef tops, in lagoons, and on outreefs with caves and crevices. Also lives in brackish water. Juveniles are common but are usually concealed in hiding places. Adults move to deeper waters of up to 150 m, although they are also found at 1–40 m.
Distribution: Red Sea to French Polynesia

Comet
Plesiopidae

The comet is the most widespread of the
roughly 20 species in this family, and is
a favourite in marine aquaria thanks to
its attractive colouring. However, comets
in general are rare. Species in the genus
Assessor are mouth breeders: the male
incubates the eggs in his mouth until
they hatch.

Comet
Calloplesiops altivelis

Length: 20 cm
Biology: Relatively common and
widespread, but lives in hiding
inside crevices. Timid. Emerges
only at sunset. Its white spots
become more numerous and
smaller with age; 3–45 m.
Distribution: Red Sea to French
Polynesia

Dottybacks
Pseudochromidae

Dottybacks are a family of small but highly colourful species. Most belong to the genus *Pseudochromis* and are timid, living in concealment in hiding places. They are seldom seen by divers even though they are not rare. All species hold small territories which they defend aggressively.

Sunrise dottyback
Pseudochromis flavivertex

Length: 7 cm
Biology: The males are blue with a broad yellow stripe at the top, while the females are yellow-coloured all over, and live a more concealed life so are rarely seen. Usually lives in sandy or gravel areas at the base of reef blocks. Timid and cautious, but frequently moves several metres away from its base.
Distribution: Red Sea, Gulf of Aden

Bigeyes
Priacanthidae

Their red colouring and, above all, their large
eyes are indicators of their nocturnal lifestyle.
During the day they often float without
moving in sheltered spots such as ledges.
In some areas, notably in the Maldives, they
are also frequently seen in large groups out
in the open, close to the seabed.

Crescent-tail bigeye
Priacanthus hamrur

Length: 40 cm
Biology: Often on outreefs,
typically in the vicinity of shelters
such as caves and crevices.
Individually or in small, informal
groups, not particularly timid.
Nocturnal, eats zooplankton in
open water. Able to change colour
instantly from bright red to silver
flecks to uniform pale silver; 10 m
to more than 100 m.
Distribution: Red Sea to French
Polynesia

Anthias
Anthiinae

Eye-catching: Anthias are relatively small but are magnificently coloured in many shades of red, violet, orange and yellow. They also form large groups – sometimes huge accumulations of more than 2,000 fish. These dense, pulsating masses of fish in constant movement are one of nature's most impressive spectacles. Always staying close to the reef, these agile diurnal fish catch zooplankton in open water. When disturbed they swim towards the reef, where they seek shelter from danger, and also at night, in crevices in the coral.

Anthias are typically found in groups containing many females, even more juveniles, but only a few males: the anthias grouping that forms the basic unit of the larger groups is a harem. Depending on species, each male can have several females and even as many as 30. The males are slightly larger and develop from high-status females by a sex-change process. When they change sex they also develop new and brighter colouring.

Scalefin anthias
Pseudanthias squamipinnis

Length: 15 cm
Biology: Forms large, frequently conspicuous groups in front of reef crests, steep slopes and drop-offs. The male of this species has an elongated dorsal fin ray, and guards a harem of between 5 and 10 females; 0.3–35 m.
Distribution: Red Sea to Fiji and south Japan

Red Sea anthias
Pseudanthias taeniatus

Length: 13 cm
Biology: *See* photo for male colouring; female is orange with a light belly. Forms harem groups of up to 15 females; likes deep habili reefs, with the females close to the bottom and the males often several metres above them. Red Sea anthias often join up with groups of other anthia species; 12–50 m.
Distribution: Red Sea

Groupers
Serranidae

Close to home: Groupers are solitary and territorial. Most of these powerful bottom-feeding fish live on coral reefs and rocky seabeds, where the rough texture of the terrain gives them perfect cover. Their territories include sheltered hiding places such as caves, crevices and ledges, and here they spend a large part of the day. However, some patrol the reef more or less in the open, even during the day.

Surprise tactics: All groupers are predators, and are one of the largest and most common predator species on the reef. They feed mainly on crustaceans, fish and squid, and their best hunting period is at twilight. In spite of their rather stout appearance, groupers can dart forwards with astonishing speed, and can seize, from a standstill, fish that are faster and more agile than themselves. Pursuit, on the other hand, is not their strong point, and offers them little chance of success.

The larger grouper species can live for between 20 and 40 years.

Coral grouper
Cephalopholis miniata

Length: 40 cm
Biology: Common, not timid. Prefers large, coral-rich lagoons and outreefs; 1–50 m.
Distribution: Red Sea to French Polynesia

Saddle grouper
Cephalopholis sexmaculata

Length: 50 cm
Biology: Lives in clear coastal and outer reefs, mostly spends the day in caves or swimming headfirst and face-down on reef tops or walls; 3–150 m.
Distribution: Red Sea to French Polynesia

Blacktip grouper
Epinephelus fasciatus

Length: 40 cm
Biology: Like the other species, its colouring depends greatly on the background: pale cream to deep reddish-brown; 1–160 m.
Distribution: Red Sea to French Polynesia

Roving coral grouper
Plectropomus pessuliferus

Length: 110 cm
Biology: Common in the Red Sea. Patrols the reef slowly, also during the day. The panther grouper (*P. p. pessuliferus*) is its sister subspecies found from the Indian Ocean to Fiji; 3–50 m.
Distribution: Red Sea

Malabar grouper
Epinephelus malabaricus

Length: 120 cm
Biology: Rare in places. Lies in wait in reef channels or at the base of the reef above sand and gravel; eats crayfish, fish and squid. Timid and cautious, a valued edible fish; 2–100 m.
Distribution: Red Sea to Tonga

Potato grouper
Epinephelus tukula

Length: 200 cm
Biology: Prefers clear, coral-rich areas. Individually or in small groups. Mostly rare, only seen in a few places; allows divers to come very close and can also often be fed; 3–150 m.
Distribution: Red Sea to Great Barrier Reef

Yellow-edged lyretail
Variola louti

Length: 80 cm
Biology: Patrols the reef slowly, also during the day. A prowling predator, it attempts to get very close to its prey. Common, not very timid. Juveniles are a different colour and live in hiding; 1–150 m.
Distribution: Red Sea to French Polynesia

Hawkfish
Cirrhitidae

A seat with a view: Hawkfish swim rarely, and then only for very short distances. They are ground-based and have no swim bladder. Most of the time they perch on a preferred vantage point, resting on their powerful pectoral fins. They like to do this on exposed coral promontories, which gives them their other popular name, the coral watchman. The name 'hawkfish' is likewise related to this habit. Like a bird of prey, they keep watch on their surroundings from a perch, diving down rapidly on passing prey – mainly shrimps and small fish. Hawkfish are protogynous hermaphrodites: they initially reach sexual maturity as females, but can later change into males if necessary. The male then often builds up a harem of several females, which he guards carefully.

Freckled hawkfish
Paracirrhites forsteri

Length: 22 cm
Biology: Colour variable, typically marked with small dark spots on the head. Feeds mainly on small fish and shrimps; 1–40 m.
Distribution: Red Sea to Polynesia

Arc-eye hawkfish
Paracirrhites arcatus

Length: 14 cm
Biology: Typically on small, branched coral colonies such as *Pocillopora* and *Stylophora*. Eats small crustaceans; 1–35 m.
Distribution: East Africa, Maldives to Polynesia

Longnose hawkfish
Oxycirrhites typus

Length: 13 cm
Biology: Usually lives in gorgonian or black coral. Its 'tartan' pattern and snout are unmistakable. Eats plankton crustaceans; 5–70 m.
Distribution: Red Sea to Panama

Cardinalfish
Apogonidae

Cardinalfish are small fish, rarely more than 12 cm in length. Most species are active at twilight and after dark. They are slow swimmers, and live close to the seabed in a small territorial area. During the day they float quietly, preferably in cracks, among branched corals. Sometimes they stay out in the open, but always close to a coral block or a rock.

At twilight they leave their hiding places. Most of them then hunt for zooplankton, while others also eat small fish and bottom-dwelling crustaceans. The tiger cardinalfish has large fangs and feeds mainly on fish.

Mouth protection: In the *Apogon* species, mating is preceded by a courtship ritual. After spawning, the fertilized eggs are collected by the male and incubated in his highly extendible mouth cavity for approximately one week. Here the eggs are protected from predators and are aerated by water rich in oxygen. During this very effective incubation period the male takes no food.

Ring-tailed cardinalfish
Apogon aureus

Length: 12 cm
Biology: Active by day, in sheltered reefs, often in large groups close to shelter; 1–40 m.
Distribution: East Africa, Maldives to Tonga

Five-lined cardinalfish
Cheilodipterus quinquelineatus

Length: 12 cm
Biology: In small groups close to hiding places among coral or rocks, or sheltering in long-spined sea urchins; 1–40 m.
Distribution: Red Sea to French Polynesia

Tiger cardinalfish
Cheilodipterus macrodon

Length: 25 cm
Biology: Floats individually or in small groups in the shelter of caves or ledges. Common, not timid; 0.5–40 m.
Distribution: Red Sea to French Polynesia

Jacks
Carangidae

Jacks are skilled hunters of the open sea, but they are regularly seen by divers since many species like to spend time close to the coast and to reefs.

Fast-response team: These nimble predators are active by day and night, and are constantly on the move. They have to do this because they have only a rudimentary swim bladder, and would sink if they stayed still. Their narrow tailstock with a deeply forked caudal fin shows that they are untiring, high-speed hunters. Fish are at the top of their menu, and sometimes it is possible to see and admire the impressive speeds they reach when hunting. Some species circle slowly in shoals in open water close to the reef. Many of these silver predators are sought-after edible species, and in some places they are very important commercially. Juveniles of some species make use of jellyfish as protection when they are out in open sea that is otherwise devoid of shelter. Young golden trevally are also well known as 'pilot fish' because they accompany sharks, among other species.

Giant trevally
Caranx ignobilis

Length: 170 cm
Biology: Individually or in small groups, often on patrol in front of escarpments; juveniles in schools; 5–80 m.
Distribution: Red Sea to French Polynesia

Orange-spotted trevally
Carangoides bajad

Length: 53 cm
Biology: Often in small groups at regular spots towards the top of the reef by day; yellow variant common in the Red Sea; 1–90 m.
Distribution: Red Sea to Indonesia

Golden trevally
Gnathanodon speciosus

Length: 110 cm
Biology: Juveniles yellow with black bars, adults in deep lagoons and on outreefs; 1–50 m.
Distribution: Red Sea to Panama

Snappers
Lutjanidae

Hunters: Snappers are reef-dwelling fish that remain close to the seabed, and are mostly inactive by day, when they remain individually or in small groups in sheltered places, such as under ledges. They are also frequently seen in sizeable groups near the seabed out in the open. In many reefs, these massive, stationary shoals of snappers are one of the most spectacular sights for divers. Fully-grown specimens of some of the larger species are solitary. Snappers are nocturnal predators, feeding primarily on bottom-dwelling invertebrates, especially crustaceans, and on squid, small fish and plankton species. The species that feed mainly on fish are readily recognizable by their fangs.

Hunted: The snapper family is a large one with more than 100 species. They are found all over the world – in tropical and sub-tropical regions and also in the Atlantic and the Caribbean. Many are important and valuable edible fish; in some areas, however, certain species can cause ciguatera poisoning, and must not be eaten in those regions.

Humpback snapper
Lutjanus gibbus

Length: 50 cm
Biology: Often in large, stationary shoals during the day. Hunts alone at night for crustaceans; 1–150 m.
Distribution: Red Sea to French Polynesia

Bluestripe snapper
Lutjanus kasmira

Length: 35 cm
Biology: Individually, in small groups or in massive shoals. Hunts at night for small fish and crustaceans; 10–264 m.
Distribution: Red Sea to French Polynesia

Midnight snapper
Macolor macularis

Length: 55 cm
Biology: Eats mostly large zooplankton; juveniles have a striking black-and-white pattern and elongated fins; 3–50 m.
Distribution: Maldives to Solomon Islands

Fusiliers
Caesionidae

Fusiliers are closely related to the snappers, but live more in the open sea, where they feed on zooplankton. They therefore have a small mouth and, because of their open-water habitat, a more streamlined body with a deeply-forked caudal fin. One single fish seems not to be a memorable sight, but these fish are very familiar to divers even if their name is not well known.

By the shoal: In many areas the great shoals of fusiliers form a large proportion of the sea's abundance. By day these skilful, untiring swimmers rest in large numbers in open water. They live by the steep slopes of outreefs, and also in lagoons. Being surrounded by these fish when descending or ascending is always an experience for a diver. During the night, the fish sleep on the reef, hidden in cracks and holes, and often take on a reddish nocturnal colouring. During the day, they seek out a reef, where they visit cleaner stations. Fusiliers are sought-after edible fish, and there are about 20 different species.

Bluestreak fusilier
Pterocaesio tile

Length: 25 cm
Biology: Hunts for zooplankton in open water, sometimes in large shoals. Rests at night in crevices and cavities, when its lower body turns red (see photo); 5–25 m.
Distribution: East Africa to Polynesia

Red Sea fusilier
Caesio suevica

Length: 25 cm
Biology: Tail has striking black and white tips. In large shoals in open water close to reefs, feeds on zooplankton. Common and curious, will often surround divers. Visits cleaner stations; 1–25 m.
Distribution: Red Sea

Yellowback fusilier
Caesio xanthonota

Length: 30 cm
Biology: Swims in large schools in the open waters of deep lagoons, and along outreefs. There are several similar species with dorsal stripes of differing lengths; 0.5–50 m
Distribution: Southern Red Sea, Maldives to the Maluku Islands

Sweetlips
Haemulidae

Daydreamers: During the day, sweetlips rest quietly in the water – alone, in small groups, some also in large shoals. They show little fear, and many species are attractively coloured. Some like to be in the open, and even in exposed locations, while others prefer more sheltered areas and remain beneath table corals or ledges. Many species have thick, fleshy lips, although members of the *Haemulon* genus do not. Juveniles are frequently a completely different colour, and some of them swim round alone, sometimes with tumbling or rippling movements, in contrast to the calm behaviour of the adults.

Sweetlips become active at night, and go individually in search of food. Their principal food is bottom-dwelling invertebrates, and they use their molars to crush crustaceans, molluscs, snails or sea urchins. They also eat worms and small fish. Some sweetlips also hunt for zooplankton in open water. The family includes about 120 species, many of which are popular edible fish.

Giant sweetlips
Plectorhinchus albovittatus

Length: 90 cm
Biology: A large species; lagoons and reef slopes, individually or in small groups by day; 1–30 m.
Distribution: Red Sea to Sri Lanka

Many-spotted sweetlips
Plectorhinchus chaetodonoides

Length: 70 cm
Biology: In coral-rich reefs, under ledges by day. Juveniles brown with white spots and a tumbling swimming action; 1–40 m.
Distribution: Maldives to Fiji

Oriental sweetlips
Plectorhinchus vittatus

Length: 86 cm
Biology: Coral-rich outreefs, adults often in small groups in sheltered or completely open locations; 2–30 m.
Distribution: East Africa to Samoa

Emperor fish
Lethrinidae

Many of the species in this family are a silvery-grey colour with no obvious pattern, so they are difficult for divers to identify. Emperor fish also have widely varying body shapes: some, for example, have a steeply sloping face, while others have a pointed head.

Smaller species, such as the striped large-eye sea bream, often live in small groups, while larger fish like the yellowfin emperor are mostly solitary. In many species the adults and juveniles are markedly different in colour. They feed mainly on bottom-dwelling invertebrates such as crustaceans and worms, and also on small fish and, in some cases, plankton. Many species are able to change colour within seconds depending on their mood, and in particular can become lighter or darker. Young humpnose big-eye bream have dark bands, which they can 'switch' on and off.

Most species feed at night, but some feed during the day, and many are active by both day and night. All species are sequential hermaphrodites, reaching sexual maturity initially as females and then becoming males later in life.

Humpnose big-eye bream
Monotaxis grandoculis

Length: 60 cm
Biology: Common, individually or in loose groups, during the day mostly float without moving at the edge of the reef; 1–100 m.
Distribution: Red Sea to Polynesia and Sumbawa

Striped large-eye bream
Gnathodentex aurolineatus

Length: 30 cm
Biology: Common, not timid, spends the day mostly in small groups but also, more rarely, in large assemblies close to coral blocks; 1–30 m.
Distribution: East Africa to Polynesia

Yellowfin emperor
Lethrinus erythracanthus

Length: 70 cm
Biology: A particularly attractive species. Solitary, timid. Likes to spend the day under or close to a ledge. Feeds on hard-shelled invertebrates; 12–120 m.
Distribution: East Africa to Polynesia

False snappers
Nemipteridae

False snappers are interval swimmers:
they swim a short distance, then float
motionless above the seabed, catch small
invertebrates and sometimes bottom-
dwelling fish, then swim a little further,
scanning the ground for food, then stand
still again for a while. In some areas they
are an important food source.

Bridled monocle bream
Scolopsis bilineatus

Length: 23 cm
Biology: Adults are solitary
and live close to sandy areas
in lagoons and sheltered
reefs. Probably a sequential
hermaphrodite like all false
snappers: females can change into
males later in life. The juveniles
imitate the poisonous fanged
blenny; 1–25 m.
Distribution: Laccadives and
Maldives to Fiji

Seabream
Sparidae

There are only a few seabream species in
the Indo-Pacific, and they are most likely to
be seen in the Indian Ocean. They are also
relatively timid here and difficult to approach.
They are present in far greater numbers and
with more species in the Atlantic, Caribbean
and Mediterranean, where they also play a
greater ecological role.

Twobar seabream
Acanthopagrus bifasciatus

Length: 50 cm
Biology: A wary and timid species,
but frequently seen around the
Red Sea. Lives on reef slopes in
deep lagoons. More common at
high tide on reef tops, and likes to
be on or in front of outreef edges
with a strong swell and surf.
Swims alone, or also frequently in
small groups; 0.2–20 m.
Distribution: Red Sea, Arabian
Gulf to Mauritius

Hatchetfish
Pempheridae

During the day they remain under ledges, in cavities, in the shelter of large coral blocks and also in wrecks – the brownish *Pempheris* species with their hatchet-shaped bodies, and the slender, transparent *Parapriacanthus* species. The latter form impressive, stationary shoals. At night they hunt individually for zooplankton in open water.

Glassy sweeper
Parapriacanthus ransonneti

Length: 10 cm
Biology: Not timid. Feeds at night on zooplankton across the reef. During the day it is possible to observe the large, dense shoals and study the shoal behaviour of fish at close quarters. In a spectacular fashion, they move out of the way of predators or divers in a pulsating mass, often forming a hollow space and then joining up again; 0.3–40 m.
Distribution: Red Sea to the Marshall Islands and New Caledonia

Moonfish
Monodactylidae

The five species in this family live mainly in estuaries and mangrove regions. They are tolerant of fluctuations in salinity, and are able to survive in fresh water. They frequently swim in large schools, close to the shore and in turbid water. They feed on small fish and invertebrates. The only species likely to be seen while diving is the silver moonfish.

Silver moonfish
Monodactylus argenteus

Length: 22 cm
Biology: Resembles the batfish but is not related to it. These attractive fish live in calm waters, mainly in brackish rivers, deltas and lagoons but also in sheltered coastal reefs. Lives mostly in a school, not very timid; 0–15 m.
Distribution: Red Sea to Samoa

Mullet
Mullidae

There are about 55 species of mullet, all of which have two barbels on the chin. These can be held flat in an episternal notch under the chin, while swimming for example, and are then almost invisible. The barbels are organs of touch and are densely covered with taste buds. Their purpose is to find food. Mullet search the sandy seabed with their barbels outstretched, unearthing small creatures in the ground. They frequently dig their prey out from deep in the sand. Their food sources include crustaceans, molluscs, brittle stars and fish. Some species also use their barbels as a whip to drive fish out from crevices or from between the branches of the coral.

Dining companions: When mullet stir up the seabed they often attract other fish, such as wrasses and emperor fish. These fish follow the mullet and catch bottom-dwelling creatures flushed out by the agitation. Although they are the only ones to benefit from the mullet's search for food, they do no harm to the mullet. This type of relationship is known as commensalism.

Red Sea goatfish
Parupeneus forsskali

Length: 28 cm
Biology: Common, active by day, not timid. Often in the company of other fish, especially wrasses; 1–30 m.
Distribution: Red Sea, Gulf of Aden

Yellowfin goatfish
Mulloidichthys vanicolensis

Length: 38 cm
Biology: Common, not timid. Nocturnal, often spends the day in large groups on reef slopes; 1–50 m.
Distribution: Red Sea to Polynesia

Manybar goatfish
Parupeneus multifasciatus

Length: 35 cm
Biology: Individually or in groups, mostly diurnal. Colour variable but always very intense; 1–140 m.
Distribution: Cocos Islands to Hawaii and Polynesia

Butterflyfish
Chaetodontidae

Bright colours: With their poster-bright colours, butterflyfish are a perfect example of vividly coloured coral fish. Their bodies are flattened laterally and are almost disc-shaped, giving them the perfect shape for manoeuvring nimbly among the coral.

Two by two: Many species of butterflyfish live in pairs, and in some species this bond is for life. Others that live in pairs have a looser bond and are frequently seen on their own. Finally, some butterflyfish, such as the schooling bannerfish, gather in large groups or shoals. This is thought to be a defensive behaviour: these species feed on plankton in the open water in front of a reef, and a shoal provides safety from predators.

Sociable: Many butterflyfish are territorial and defend their space against others of the same species. These disputes can become quite heated, but are mostly limited to ritualistic behaviour, which includes staring, darting rapidly towards each other, chasing, bolting and circling. It is rare for this to escalate into actual fighting.

Spotted butterflyfish
Chaetodon guttatissimus

Length: 12 cm
Biology: Moves across the reef in pairs or in small groups. Its food is mainly worms, coral polyps and algae; 2–25 m.
Distribution: East Africa, Maldives to western Thailand

White collar butterflyfish
Chaetodon collare

Length: 16 cm
Biology: Not very timid. Swims in pairs, frequently also hovering in small, stationary groups in front of coral bommies. Feeds on coral polyps and worms; 1–20 m.
Distribution: Gulf of Aden, Maldives to the Philippines

Scrawled butterflyfish
Chaetodon meyeri

Length: 18 cm
Biology: Usually in pairs, territorial. Feeds only on coral polyps. Juveniles mainly in the shelter of horn corals; 2–25 m.
Distribution: East Africa, Maldives to Polynesia

Threadfin butterflyfish
Chaetodon auriga

Length: 23 cm
Biology: Common, not timid, widespread. Individually, in pairs or in small groups. Picks off bits of coral polyp, small worms, anemones and algae; 1–35 m.
Distribution: Red Sea to French Polynesia

Bennett's butterflyfish
Chaetodon bennetti

Length: 18 cm
Biology: Individually or in pairs, prefers coral-rich lagoons and outreefs. Feeds on coral polyps. Juveniles can be seen among the branches of horn corals; 5–30 m.
Distribution: East Africa, Maldives to Pitcairn Islands

Melon butterflyfish
Chaetodon trifasciatus

Length: 15 cm
Biology: Usually lives in pairs, and is territorial. An extremely specialized feeder, it eats only coral polyps; 1–20 m.
Distribution: East Africa, Maldives to French Polynesia

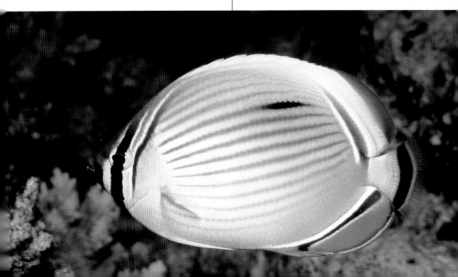

Red-back butterflyfish
Chaetodon paucifasciatus

Length: 14 cm
Biology: Lives in pairs or small groups. Common and not timid. Has a large home territory. Its preferred food is stone corals and soft corals; 1–30 m.
Distribution: Endemic to Red Sea and Gulf of Aden

Masked butterflyfish
Chaetodon semilarvatus

Length: 23 cm
Biology: Mostly in pairs, sometimes in groups. Hovers under table corals during the day, and especially before noon. Common and not timid; 3–20 m.
Distribution: Endemic to Red Sea and Gulf of Aden

Longnose butterflyfish
Forcipiger flavissimus

Length: Up to 22 cm
Biology: Roams in pairs or small groups, mainly on outreefs. Not timid. Wide range of food sources, also picks off the feet of sea urchins or starfish; 2–110 m.
Distribution: Red Sea to Central America

Schooling bannerfish
Heniochus diphreutes

Length: 18 cm
Biology: Lives on outreefs. Sometimes feeds in large groups on plankton in open water in front of an outreef. Prefers areas with rising deepwater currents that are rich in plankton; 5–210 m.
Distribution: Red Sea to Hawaii

Angelfish
Pomacanthidae

Visible from far away because of their vivid poster colours, the larger angelfish in particular move almost majestically across the reef. They are territorial: large *Pomacanthus* species have a territory of more than 1,000 square metres, while the smaller *Centropyge* species patrol an area of only a few square metres.

Changing clothes: The young of the Indo-Pacific *Pomacanthus* species all look very similar – dark blue to almost black, with white stripes. However, when they mature they undergo a dramatic colour change, and when this is complete the 'Emperor's new clothes' are completely different from the juvenile form.

Changing sex: Angelfish mature sexually as females initially, but can subsequently change sex and become males (protogynous hermaphrodites). In most species, there is no difference in colour between the sexes, although an exception is the *Genicanthus* genus, in which males and females can sometimes differ quite markedly in their colouring.

Arabian angelfish
Pomacanthus maculosus

Length: 50 cm
Biology: Individually but also sometimes in pairs. Not timid. This is one of the largest species. Its food includes sponges, leather corals and algae; 2–60 m.
Distribution: Red Sea, Arabian peninsula to the Seychelles

Emperor angelfish
Pomacanthus imperator

Length: 40 cm
Biology: Prefers coral-rich deep lagoons, coastal reefs and outreefs. Has a large home territory. Mostly individually or in pairs, occasionally also in a harem. Feeds on sponges, sea squirts, cnidarians and algae; 3–80 m.
Distribution: Red Sea to French Polynesia

Regal angelfish
Pygoplites diacanthus

Length: 25 cm
Biology: Individually or in pairs; relatively common but timid, and hurries away from divers into cracks and holes, near which it spends most of its time. Feeds on sponges and sea squirts; 1–80 m.
Distribution: Red Sea to French Polynesia

Blue-girdled angelfish
Pomacanthus narvachus

Length: 28 cm
Biology: Mostly individually, often close to its hiding place, relatively timid. Feeds principally on sponges and sea squirts. Rarely seen except in Indonesia; 3–30 m.
Distribution: Indonesia to the Philippines and New Guinea

Threespot angelfish
Apolemichthys trimaculatus

Length: 25 cm
Biology: Frequently on steep, coral-rich reef slopes; individually or in pairs, relatively timid. Feeds primarily on sponges and sea squirts. Juveniles live below 25 m and are well concealed; 3–40 m.
Distribution: East Africa, Maldives to Samoa

Zebra lyretail angelfish
Genicanthus caudovittatus

Length: Up to 20 cm
Biology: Usually in harem groups consisting of a male and between 5 and 9 females. Feeds mainly on zooplankton. Male has zebra stripes, female plain pale grey; 15–70 m (usually below 25 m).
Distribution: Red Sea to Maldives

Damselfish
Pomacentridae

Minor role-players: Damselfish liven things up with their numerous species and large numbers, together with their bustling lively behaviour. Reefs would be a great deal poorer without the damselfish. Yet, despite their importance within the reef community, they often receive little attention from divers, who consider damselfish to be merely the bit players on the stage of the coral reef.

This successful family contains more than 320 species and lives mainly in tropical waters. Their food is often plankton or algae, but some species are omnivorous. Most species remain quite small at less than 10 cm in length: the Indo-Pacific sergeant, which can reach 20 cm, is considered one of the largest members of the family. This species is ideal for divers to observe the typical breeding behaviour of the damselfish. First, a spot is chosen on a firm area of ground, and is then scrupulously cleaned. More than a thousand sticky eggs (depending on species) are laid on this spot. The clutch of eggs is then guarded until the fish hatch out, and oxygen-rich water is fanned over it.

Golden damselfish
Amblyglyphidodon aureus

Length: 14 cm
Biology: Catches zooplankton in open water; prefers to live on outreefs; 3–45 m.
Distribution: Cocos Islands to Fiji

Indo-Pacific sergeant
Abudefduf vaigiensis

Length: 20 cm
Biology: In shoals, preferably on outer edges of the reef, where it feeds on plankton; 0.3–12 m
Distribution: Red Sea to French Polynesia

Green chromis
Chromis viridis

Length: 9 cm
Biology: In small shoals on *Acropora* branch coral, into which it bolts at the slightest danger; 0.5–12 m.
Distribution: Red Sea to French Polynesia

Anemone fish
Amphiprioninae

Bed of nettles: Without their anemone hosts they would be easy prey for their many predators. Anemone fish live close together among the stinging cells of the tentacles, and also snuggle down there for the night. They acquire an immunity to the stings when they are young by initially touching the tentacles very cautiously, but other animals suffer stings. Anemone fish fiercely defend their anemone against fish who might want to eat the tentacles, and are sometimes even daring enough to try and drive away divers, who they think might be hostile to the anemone.

Girl power: The largest and socially dominant fish in an anemone is always a female, and her immediate subordinate a male. These two form a permanent pair bond. Any other anemone fish living alongside this pair are invariably young ones. If the female dies, the highest-ranking male undergoes a sex change within a week and becomes the dominant female.

False clown anemone fish
Amphiprion ocellaris

Length: 9 cm
Biology: Lagoons and sheltered outreefs. Often in small groups on one anemone. Present on three host anemones, including the magnificent anemone (*Heteractis magnifica*) as shown in the photo; 1–15 m.
Distribution: Andaman Sea to the Philippines and north-west Australia

Clark's anemone fish
Amphiprion clarkii

Length: 14 cm
Biology: A variety of colour variants, mostly black with varying amounts of orange in the head area. The most widely distributed of all the anemone fish. Present on all 10 species of host anemone; 1–55 m.
Distribution: Arabian Gulf, Maldives to south Japan and Fiji

Maldives anemone fish
Amphiprion nigripes

Length: 11 cm
Biology: Small area of distribution; lives exclusively on the magnificent anemone (*Heteractis magnifica*); 1–25 m.
Distribution: Maldives, Sri Lanka

Pink anemone fish
Amphiprion perideraion

Length: 10 cm
Biology: Lives on the magnificent anemone, more rarely with three other host anemones; 3–30 m.
Distribution: South-east Thailand, Malaysia and Cocos Islands to Samoa

Cinnamon clownfish
Amphiprion melanopus

Length: 12 cm
Biology: Frequently in large colonies, lives on three different anemone species; 1–18 m.
Distribution: Sulawesi and Maluku Islands to French Polynesia

Spinecheek anemone fish
Premnas biaculeatus

Length: 11 cm, rarely up to 16 cm
Biology: Lives exclusively on a single anemone species (*Entacmaea quadricolor*); 1–16 m.
Distribution: Western Indonesia to the Great Barrier Reef and Vanuatu

Wrasses
Labridae

This family is made up of about 500 species and has a characteristic swimming motion: forward movement is achieved using the pectoral fins only, and the tailfin is used only for high-speed swimming – when escaping, for example. These fish are active by day, often vividly coloured, and most of the smaller species are also agile swimmers. At night, the smaller species usually bury themselves in the sand, while the larger fish normally find a sheltered spot to rest in.

New clothes: All wrasses are thought to be sequential hermaphrodites: mature females are able to change into males later in life. In many species, different ages and genders can be distinguished by colour.

Cleaning team: Cleaner wrasses maintain cleaning stations where parasites and loose skin flakes are removed from the bodies of other fish. During this process the 'clients' usually remain still in the water, letting the cleaners into their mouths and between their gills. This skin hygiene makes an important contribution to the health of the client fish and provides the cleaners with their food.

Humphead wrasse
Cheilinus undulatus

Length: 230 cm
Biology: The largest of the wrasses, weighing up to 190 kg. Timid by nature but in many areas has become accustomed to divers. Not common anywhere, it is solitary and has a large territory. It eats loricate invertebrates such as snails, molluscs and sea urchins. Heavily depleted in some areas because of its popularity in South-east Asian restaurants; 1–60 m.
Distribution: Red Sea to French Polynesia

Broomtail wrasse
Cheilinus lunulatus

Length: 50 cm
Biology: Usually solitary, on coral-rich reef edges with sand and gravel areas. Feeds mainly on bottom-dwelling invertebrates such as crustaceans, snails and molluscs. Spawns during the afternoon at high tide along the edges of the reef: one male lives with a harem of several females; 0.5–30 m.
Distribution: Red Sea to Arabian Gulf

Bandcheek wrasse
Oxycheilinus diagrammus

Length: 35 cm
Biology: In coral-rich lagoons and outreefs;
often swims long distances across the
seabed. A predator on small fish. Not timid,
sometimes can even be curious; 2–60 m.
Distribution: Red Sea to Samoa

Sixbar wrasse
Thalassoma hardwicke

Length: 20 cm
Biology: Shallow, coral-rich lagoons and
outreefs with clear water; frequently up on
the reef top. Feeds on invertebrates and
small fish from the seabed and open water;
1–15 m.
Distribution: East Africa to Polynesia

Checkerboard wrasse
Halichoeres hortulanus

Length: 27 cm
Biology: An agile species in constant movement during the day. Frequent in clear lagoons and outreefs. Feeds on bottom-dwelling invertebrates. The male has a large territory; 1–30 m.
Distribution: Red Sea to French Polynesia

Slingjaw wrasse
Epibulus insidiator

Length: 35 cm
Biology: Coral-rich outreefs; solitary and relatively timid. Eats shrimps, crustaceans and fish. Several colour variants but female is usually plain yellow; 1–30 m.
Distribution: Red Sea to Polynesia

Parrotfish
Scaridae

Stone biters: Parrotfish are attractive to look at – and can often also be heard. They use their beak-like mouths to scrape minute algae from rocks and coral, causing a scratching sound that can be heard over a considerable distance. They also scrape at living coral to obtain the symbiotic algae in the top layers of the skeleton. Some will bite off entire branches from branch corals, grinding them between their millstone-like pharyngeal teeth.

Many colours: Parrotfish can change sex from female to male during their lives, when they also change colour. Older males can have very vivid colouring; juveniles, too, often have a distinctive colour.

Sleeping bag: Parrotfish are frequently seen during night dives, asleep under ledges or wedged into crevices. Some species also cover themselves with a transparent cocoon of mucus, which acts as a scent barrier and protects them from nocturnal predators like moray eels which detect their prey by scent.

Humphead parrotfish
Bolbometapon muricatum

Length: 130 cm
Biology: The largest species of the family, grows up to weigh at least 70 kg. Feeds on living coral, from which it bites off entire branches. Also eats algae. Sleeps at night in a group inside large crevices and caves. Timid, and rare in most areas; 1–50 m.
Distribution: Red Sea to French Polynesia

Roundhead parrotfish
Scarus strongylocephalus

Length: 70 cm
Biology: Common, widespread and relatively large species. Swims alone or in pairs in lagoons and on outreefs. Adults are also very rarely seen patrolling in shoals. Females have reddish undersides and yellow-green backs; 2–35 m.
Distribution: Gulf of Aden to south-west Indonesia

Rusty parrotfish
Scarus ferrugineus

Length: 40 cm
Biology: Male is blue with green, female brownish with a yellow tail. Common, not timid. Male is territorial and has a harem consisting of several females. Covers itself with a slimy cocoon at night; 1–60 m.
Distribution: Red Sea to Arabian Gulf

Bullethead parrotfish
Chlororus sordidus

Length: 40 cm
Biology: A very common species, not timid. Lives in lagoons, on reef tops and outreefs; juveniles frequently on seaweed and gravel. Can sometimes travel long distances during the day between its feeding and sleeping places; 1–30 m.
Distribution: Red Sea to Polynesia

Longnose parrotfish
Hipposcarus harid

Length: 75 cm
Biology: Deep lagoons, coves and semi-sheltered outreefs. Often on sand and gravel, where it grazes on blanket weed. Frequently seen in small groups consisting of a male and several harem females; 1–30 m.
Distribution: Red Sea to Java

Bicolour parrotfish
Cetoscarus bicolor

Length: 80 cm
Biology: The juveniles (*see* photo) of this species have very distinctive colouring. They mostly swim across small sandy areas between blocks of coral, and are frequently seen by divers; 1–30 m.
Distribution: Red Sea to French Polynesia

Sandperch
Pinguididae

This predator typically lies in wait supported on its ventral fins and with its head raised slightly to give it a better view, usually on sandy areas but in some cases also on gravel, rock or coral. They dart quickly forwards to catch invertebrates and small fish. The males are territorial, and have a harem of several females.

Speckled sandperch
Parapercis hexophthalma

Length: 28 cm
Biology: Male and female sandperch can often be distinguished by slight variations in their colour pattern. This is also true of this species: the male has bands on its cheeks, while the female has dots. Feeds on bottom-dwelling invertebrates. Sleeps under gravel at night. The male has a harem of 2–5 females; spawning takes place at sunset; 2–22 m.
Distribution: Red Sea to Fiji

Sand-divers
Trichonotidae

These very elongated fish are sequential hermaphrodites: the females are able to change into males in later life. The male is identified by the thread-like spines on its dorsal fin, which it raises when mating, together with its pectoral fins. Males are territorial and have a harem. Feed on zooplankton.

Red Sea sand-diver
Trichonotus nikei

Length: 12 cm
Biology: Lives on sheltered sandy slopes in coves. Usually in a small group close to the bottom – not more than 1–3 metres above it – and feeds on zooplankton. When threatened it dives instantly head-first into the sand, where it also spends the night; 2–90 m.
Distribution: Red Sea. There are very similar species in other Indo-Pacific regions.

Tuna and mackerel
Scombridae

Tuna are perfectly designed for speed: a spindle-shaped body that is rigid at the front and has a narrow tailstock and a tall, curved tailfin. They are the real pacemakers of the ocean, reaching top speeds of up to 95 kph. Untiring swimmers, they cover long distances in their search for food, and eat up to a quarter of their bodyweight every day.

Dogtooth tuna
Gymnosarda unicolor

Length: 220 cm
Biology: White mouth opening with large fangs. Swims alone or in small groups, patrolling open water along deep lagoons, channels and outreefs. This high-speed predator hunts in particular for fusiliers and other plankton-feeders. Not timid, occasionally even curious with divers; 1–100 m.
Distribution: Red Sea to French Polynesia

Triplefins
Tripterygiidae

Triplefins get their name from their three dorsal fins. It is the only family on the coral reef that has this distinctive feature, but it is usually difficult to identify because the fins are very close together. These tiny, elongated bottom-dwellers feed on small invertebrates of the seabed. Often overlooked, not just because of their small size but because many are very well camouflaged.

Striped triplefin
Helcogramma striatum

Length: 4 cm
Biology: This is one of the very few species that are eye-catching and attractively coloured. It is also common, and is often seen by divers. These fish like to rest on corals, sponges and other hard surfaces. They are found individually or in small groups, and will allow divers very close if approached with care; 0.5–15 m
Distribution: Indonesia to Line Islands; there is a similar species in the Maldives.

Blennies
Blenniidae

The 350 species in this family have no scales, or only very small, smooth ones; instead, they have a protective mucus coating.

Sedentary: Blennies live on hard ground and have a small burrow. They lay their eggs on the ground – in cracks, under stones, or in empty shells. The brood is often guarded by the male, and sometimes by both parents. The males have small territories, which they defend against their rivals. There are two species that live in coral reefs: combtooth blennies have small, comb-like teeth for scraping tiny blanket-weed algae from hard surfaces and eating small invertebrates. The Midas blenny eats zooplankton. Sabretooth blennies are predators with long, curved eyeteeth, and are usually active swimmers. Some specialist species bite scales, skin mucus and even pieces of fin from larger fish.

A wolf in sheep's clothing: To do this, some sabretooth blennies mimic harmless species. The false cleanerfish mimics genuine cleaner wrasses (page 104) in its colouring and swimming motion in order to get close to its victims.

Red Sea mimic blenny
Escenius gravieri

Length: 8 cm
Biology: Mimics the poisonous blackline fangblenny to protect itself from predators; 2–20 m.
Distribution: Red Sea to Gulf of Aden

Midas blenny
Escenius midas

Length: 13 cm
Biology: There are bluish-grey and yellow variants, the latter mimicking the sea goldie (page 62) and mingling with their shoals; 2–35 m.
Distribution: Red Sea to Polynesia

Bluestriped fangblenny
Plagiotremus rhinorhynchus

Length: 12 cm
Biology: Bites off scales and pieces of fin from other fish. Juveniles mimic young cleaner wrasses; 1–40 m.
Distribution: Red Sea to French Polynesia

Dragonets
Callionymidae

There are about 125 species of dragonet, making them a relatively large family, but they often go unnoticed. Most species remain very small, well below 10 cm. In addition, all dragonets are bottom-dwelling species that remain on sandy or muddy seabeds – not the diver's preferred environment. Finally, many species are able to burrow in the sand, and often do so during the day. If this were not enough, most species have the same colouring as their backgrounds, so they are well camouflaged. It would be quite possible to omit them here were it not for a few species that are spectacularly coloured and are particular favourites of photographers in many diving areas. Virtually no one wants to miss the courtship dance of the mandarin fish, one of the most popular photographic 'models'. In most dragonet species the males are more brightly coloured; mating is preceded by a lengthy courtship ritual.

Mandarin fish
Synchiropus splendidus

Length: 6 cm
Biology: Common in some areas, but hides on soft ground with thick gravel, or in coral branches. Is also present in more turbid water. They mate at sunset, when pairs swim straight up from the seabed with their bodies in close contact; 3–30 m.
Distribution: Indonesia, southern Japan, Philippines to New Guinea

Fingered dragonet
Dactylopus dactylopus

Length: 18 cm
Biology: Lives on sheltered sand or gravel ground close to a reef or near the shore. Often buried during the day; raises its dorsal fins if disturbed. Feeds on small bottom-dwelling invertebrates; 1–55 m.
Distribution: Tropical Western Pacific e.g. Philippines, Indonesia, Papua New Guinea

Gobies
Gobiidae

A big family: With more than 2,000 species, gobies are the largest family of marine fish. Most of them are small, bottom-dwelling fish without a swim bladder. Some species change sex, others do not. Many live in holes, sometimes alone and sometimes in those occupied by other creatures.

Watchdogs and builders: Some species live in a close symbiotic relationship with the snapping rock-boring shrimp. This shrimp is almost blind and digs a burrow in the sand up to 50 cm long, sometimes with more than one entrance. The goby eats minute invertebrates, including those exposed by the shrimp's digging and maintenance activities. In return for receiving shelter on a sandy seabed that otherwise provides no cover, the fish's role in the partnership is that of a watchdog. When the shrimp wishes to deposit a load of sand in the open, it always keeps one antenna in contact with the goby, which retreats deep into the burrow at the slightest disturbance, accompanied by the shrimp, which has thus been warned. A note of interest: a goby of the Maldives (*Trimmaton natans*), only 8 mm long, is the smallest vertebrate on earth.

Gold-headed sleeper goby
Valenciennea strigata

Length: 18 cm
Biology: Juveniles in groups, adults mainly in pairs and close together; 1–20 m.
Distribution: Southern Red Sea to French Polynesia

Citron goby
Gobiodon citrinus

Length: 6.5 cm
Biology: Sits in branched coral, individually or in groups. It is covered with a bitter and possibly poisonous skin mucus (protection against predators); 1–25 m.
Distribution: Red Sea to Samoa

Signal goby
Signigobius biocellatus

Length: 6.5 cm
Biology: Lives in sheltered reefs. Its 'eyes' are to frighten predators because they give the impression of great size; 1–30 m.
Distribution: Indonesia and Philippines to Solomon Islands and Great Barrier Reef

Orange-dash goby
Valenciennea puellaris

Length: 14 cm
Biology: Builds a burrow under lumps of gravel, removing the sand with its mouth. Usually in pairs at burrow entrance; darts instantly into the burrow when threatened; feeds on small invertebrates; 2–30 m.
Distribution: Red Sea to Samoa

Aurora goby
Amblyeleotris aurora

Length: 9 cm
Biology: Lives on coarse coral sand, on reef tops and shallow outreef areas. Lives in symbiosis with the snapping shrimp, *Alpheus randalli*; 1–35 m.
Distribution: East Africa to Maldives and Andaman Sea

Whipcoral goby
Bryaninops youngei

Length: 3 cm
Biology: Lives exclusively on whip coral –
two fish often live on a single coral, which
they do not leave. If disturbed, they dart
round to the other side; 3–45 m.
Distribution: Red Sea to Polynesia

Pink-eye goby
Bryaninops natans

Length: 2.5 cm
Biology: Transparent body, purple eyes.
Lagoons and sheltered reefs. Hovers in
groups across branched coral and black
coral, catches zooplankton from the
current; 7–27 m.
Distribution: Red Sea to Cook Islands

Jawfish
Opistognathidae

Jawfish have a massive head with very large eyes and mouth, but they feed on zooplankton. They use their powerful jaws to build almost vertical burrows in sand or gravel, strengthening them from the inside with small stones and fragments of coral and shell. Their homes resemble a brick-lined well, giving them the popular name of 'well-diggers'. All species are mouth breeders.

Gold-specs jawfish
Opistognathus randalli

Length: 11 cm
Biology: Spends most of the time peeping out of its burrow. After mating, the male takes the fertilized eggs in his mouth. The ball, containing hundreds of eggs, is well protected in his mouth and is supplied with fresh, oxygen-rich water. The young hatch after about 5 days, when they have to fend for themselves; 3–20 m.
Distribution: Indonesia to the Philippines

Dartfish
Ptereleotridae

Dartfish, sometimes referred to as torpedo or arrow gobies, are small, elongated fish that live on sand, gravel, scree or muddy sediment. Typically they live in pairs; some also live in small or large groups. They never move far from their shelters, into which they rush when threatened. They feed on zooplankton, which they catch from passing currents while hovering above the ground.

Fire dartfish
Nemateleotris magnifica

Length: 7 cm
Biology: Relatively common on hard ground, often in pairs but also singly or in groups; hovers close to the ground, darts into its burrow when threatened; 6–60 m.
Distribution: East Africa to Hawaii and Pitcairn Islands

Spadefish
Ephippidae

A favourite of divers and photographers. Spadefish are large, handsome and not at all timid – indeed, they can be curious and will swim round divers, especially in popular diving spots. In addition, they usually appear in photogenic groupings, sometimes even in large shoals. It is not unusual to see them at cleaner stations. They can change the brightness of their colour very quickly from silvery white to a dark smoky colour.

Falling leaves: The bodies of spadefish are flattened laterally and are disc-shaped. Their mouths are small in relation to their overall size, and they have small, brush-like teeth. Juveniles vary considerably in terms of colour and body shape. They have very elongated dorsal, anal and ventral fins, which become smaller as they grow older. The young of some species turn over sideways when threatened so that they look like leaves floating in the current.

Longfin spadefish
Platax teira

Length: 60 cm
Biology: Individually or in schools, on a reef slope or in front of it in open water. Juveniles stay close to the reef, preferring shallow, sheltered places; 1–20 m.
Distribution: Red Sea to Fiji

Circular spadefish
Platax orbicularis

Length: 57 cm
Biology: Individually or in schools, frequently along steep slopes. Juveniles are pelagic and sometimes enter coves in sheltered places such as a landing stage. Their colour and movements give them the appearance of dead leaves; 2–34 m.
Distribution: Red Sea to French Polynesia

Rabbitfish
Siganidae

Sociable: Rabbitfish move around in pairs or groups, sometimes in shoals of several hundred. About half of the roughly 30 species live in schools when young, but form pairs later. The other species remain in schools all their lives.

Rabbitfish rest at night, lying down sideways on the seabed without seeking shelter. They have the ability to change colour very quickly, and adopt camouflage colouring when sleeping, when they become a less distinct colour with marbling and flecks.

Nibblers: It is rare to see rabbitfish at rest: they spend most of their time in a ceaseless search for food. They feed mainly on algae and seaweed, and also on invertebrates such as sea squirts and sponges. When feeding, the small mouth with its thicker top lip makes characteristic nibbling movements, which is what gives them their name.

Caution: Unlikely as it seems, these inoffensive creatures have numerous poisonous spines, which they use for defence and can cause painful injuries.

Two-barred rabbitfish
Siganus virgatus

Length: 33 cm
Biology: Usually swims in pairs in shallow coastal waters; occasionally ventures into fresh water; 2–25 m.
Distribution: Southern India to West Papua

Gold-spotted rabbitfish
Siganus stellatus

Length: 40 cm
Biology: Common and not timid. Adults in pairs, juveniles in groups. Patrols a large territory, feeds on blanket weed; 1–40 m.
Distribution: Red Sea, Gulf of Aden

Golden rabbitfish
Siganus guttatus

Length: 43 cm
Biology: Juveniles frequently among seaweed, adults form small schools on coastal reefs; 2–15 m.
Distribution: Andaman Sea to West Papua

Surgeonfish
Acanthuridae

This family is divided into scalpel, unicorn and saw surgeonfish. Most of the first group graze minute blanketweed algae from rocks. Others, especially the *Naso* species, feed on zooplankton. Like other algae-feeders, the grazing surgeonfish play an important role in the ecological balance of the reef. An experiment was carried out in which nets were used to keep algae-feeding fish away from particular parts of a reef. Within a very short time, these areas experienced an explosive growth of blanket weed that overran the coral and had a serious negative impact.

Stilettos: The sharp blades of bone on each side of the tailstock are what gives the family its name. Scalpel surgeonfish have a blade on each side, which fits into a groove. When they turn their tails sideways, the blade on the outer curve of the tail jumps out like a switchblade. Unicorn and saw surgeonfish, however, have fixed blades.

Powderblue surgeonfish
Acanthurus leucosternon

Length: 23 cm
Biology: Lives on clearwater outreef tops; singly, sometimes also in large groups; 1–25 m.
Distribution: East Africa to West Indonesia

Yellowmask surgeonfish
Acanthurus mata

Length: 50 cm
Biology: Frequently found in groups at the edge of a reef. Changes colour at cleaner stations; 5–45 m.
Distribution: Red Sea to French Polynesia

Sohal surgeonfish
Acanthurus sohal

Length: 40 cm
Biology: Frequently seen at the edge of the reef top, likes to be in the 3-m zone. The male defends a small feeding territory; 0.3–10 m.
Distribution: Red Sea to Arabian Gulf

Convict surgeonfish
Acanthurus triostegus

Length: 27 cm
Biology: Usually travels the reef in a large group and can sometimes invade the territory of other algae feeders despite its relatively small size; 1–90 m.
Distribution: East Africa to Panama

Yellowtail tang
Zebrasoma xanthurum

Length: 22 cm
Biology: Inhabits coral-rich reefs with channels and caves. Individually or in small groups. Grazes on blanket weed on dead coral, gravel and rocks; 0.5–22 m.
Distribution: Red Sea to Arabian Gulf

Sleek unicornfish
Naso hexacanthus

Length: 75 cm
Biology: A common species, usually in groups, tends not to move more than a few metres away from the reef. Feeds on large zooplankton. Able to change colour rapidly; 6–137 m.
Distribution: Red Sea to French Polynesia

Bignose unicornfish
Naso vlamingii

Length: 75 cm
Biology: Usually swims in loose groups high on the reef, hunting for large zooplankton. Changes colour dramatically and quickly at cleaner stations and during mating; 4–50 m.
Distribution: East Africa to French Polynesia

Moorish idol
Zanclidae

When glimpsed briefly, this fish could pass as a *Heniochus* (page 93, butterfly fish). However, it is not related to this species but to the surgeonfish. Apart from that it is the sole representative of its family, which consists of only one species: the moorish idol.

Moorish idol
Zanclus cornutus

Length: 22 cm
Biology: Lives on reefs of rock and coral, moves above the reef in pairs or small groups, occasionally in large schools. Feeds mainly on sponges but also on other animal and plant life. Its pelagic larval stage is very long, so it has a very wide range of distribution. It does not go to live down on the reef until it is almost fully grown; 1–145 m.
Distribution: East Africa, Maldives to Mexico

Barracudas
Sphyraenidae

Barracudas are powerful, active predators. They can accelerate very quickly – more quickly than any other marine fish – and catch their prey with a rapid forward lunge. With its powerful jaws and sharp teeth, a barracuda can easily bite in half a fish as big as itself.

Great barracuda
Sphyraena barracuda

Length: 190 cm
Biology: Juveniles often in groups, adults usually solitary. Often remains motionless in open water beside or above the reef. Curious, may approach divers, but generally not dangerous unless provoked; 1–198 m.
Distribution: Red Sea to Polynesia and tropical Atlantic

Triggerfish
Balistidae

Triggerfish prepare shallow sandy pits, where they lay their eggs. The eggs are defended against predators, and even against divers in some larger species. In this situation the diver should move away from the nest immediately. Apart from during the breeding season, even the largest species are placid.

Crunchy: Triggerfish have powerful jaws with chisel-shaped teeth, which they use to crack open even hard-shelled species such as molluscs, snails, coral, sea urchins and crustaceans. They often use a jet of water to expose prey hidden under the sand; it is mainly the larger species that use this method.

Anchored: When threatened, triggerfish escape into crevices in the reef – they do this also to rest at night. They raise the first spine on their dorsal fin to wedge themselves in.

The lower part of the second spine pushes into an indentation at its base, holding the first spine in an upright position. The fish is now securely anchored in its hiding place, and a predator would have great difficulty in pulling it out.

Picasso triggerfish
Rhinecanthus assasi

Length: 30 cm
Biology: Solitary and territorial, usually close to a hiding place. Fairly timid; 1–25 m.
Distribution: Red Sea to Arabian Gulf

Orange-lined triggerfish
Balistapus undulatus

Length: 30 cm
Biology: Makes a shallow nest pit in sand or gravel when spawning. Individually or in small groups; 1–50 m.
Distribution: Red Sea to French Polynesia

Redtoothed triggerfish
Odonus niger

Length: 40 cm
Biology: Outreefs with strong currents, frequently in large groups in open water, catching zooplankton; 3–55 m.
Distribution: Red Sea to French Polynesia

Titan triggerfish
Balistoides viridescens

Length: 75 cm
Biology: Largest species, usually solitary,
not timid. In pairs while caring for the
eggs, which it lays in a hollow in the sand.
Caution: will attack divers who get too close
to the eggs; 1–40 m.
Distribution: Red Sea to French Polynesia

Yellow-spotted triggerfish
Pseudobalistes fuscus

Length: 55 cm
Biology: Can occasionally be seen blowing
sand away with a jet of water to expose prey;
0.5–50 m.
Distribution: Red Sea to French Polynesia

Yellow-margin triggerfish
Pseudobalistes flavimarginatus

Length: 60 cm
Biology: Often in lagoons and in coves with seaweed. Feeds on coral and bottom-dwelling invertebrates, which it exposes by blowing a jet of water. May be aggressive while guarding eggs; 2–50 m.
Distribution: Red Sea to French Polynesia

Clown triggerfish
Balistoides conspicillum

Length: 50 cm
Biology: Timid and solitary, with a large territory; clear, coral-rich outreefs; juveniles are a different colour and live mainly below 20 m in areas with plenty of hiding places; 1–75 m.
Distribution: East Africa to Samoa

Filefish
Monacanthidae

Filefish swim slowly and sedately, can manoeuvre skilfully, and often hover motionless on the spot. Most of the smaller species live in concealment or camouflaged, and prefer to stay close to cover, to which they often have a similar colouring – seaweed, horn coral or soft coral. Most filefish live individually or in pairs, sometimes also in small groups, and eat a variety of foods, including algae, seaweed, sponges, worms and crustaceans. Some species, however, are genuine specialist feeders.

Rough skin: Filefish are close relatives of the triggerfish, and like them have an extended primary dorsal fin spine that can be raised and folded back. They have a tough, leathery skin with very small scales carrying minute spikes, and they feel rough like sandpaper – hence the name 'filefish'. The non-poisonous blacksaddle filefish mimics the venomous Valentin's sharpnose puffer, which it very closely resembles.

Scrawled filefish
Aluterus scriptus

Length: 100 cm
Biology: Solitary and not often seen. Juveniles live in the open sea (pelagic) in the shelter of jellyfish or seaweed; 2–80 m.
Distribution: Circumtropical

Harlequin filefish
Oxymonacanthus halli

Length: 7 cm
Biology: Feeds exclusively on *Acropora* staghorn coral; a very similar species is distributed from East Africa to Samoa; 0.3–30 m.
Distribution: Red Sea

Blacksaddle filefish
Paraluteres prionurus

Length: 11 cm
Biology: Singly or in small groups; mimics the poisonous Valentin's sharpnose puffer (page 149); 1–25 m
Distribution: Gulf of Aden, Maldives to Marshall Islands

Boxfish
Ostraciidae

Masters of manoeuvre: Boxfish are slow swimmers, but they make up for it with their manoeuvring skills. They use precision movements of their fins to turn round on the spot, rotate like a helicopter, and even swim backwards. Their precision swimming involves very little body movement – it is achieved instead by a complex interaction of their fins.

Immobile: They have no alternative, because more than three-quarters of their body length is covered by a rigid, immobile bony armour. The hard, angular external armour is made up of (mainly) hexagonal bony plates, and the honeycomb shape of the plates is readily visible in some species. As well as their armour, boxfish have another defence against predators: they secrete a highly effective toxic mucus from skin glands. These protective and warning measures frighten off many potential predators.

In many species males and females are different colours, and in some species the juveniles also (*see* photos right).

Yellow boxfish
Ostracion cubicus

Length: 45 cm
Biology: Relatively common, solitary. The large male is bluish grey with a nasal bulge (*see* photo right); 1–45 m.
Distribution: Red Sea to Polynesia

Yellow boxfish
Female

Yellow boxfish
Juvenile

The juveniles are a striking lemon yellow with black dots, and like to hide within branch coral and in other shelters.

Solor boxfish
Ostracion solorensis

Length: 11 cm
Biology: Timid, lives in hiding. Prefers coral-rich outreefs. Males have a dark blue background, females (photo) brown to green; 1–20 m.
Distribution: Indonesia to the Philippines, Papua New Guinea and Great Barrier Reef

Spotted boxfish
Ostracion meleagris

Length: 16 cm
Biology: Solitary, prefers clear lagoons and outreefs. Males develop from females who change sex (protogynous hermaphrodites); 1–30 m.
Distribution: East Africa, Maldives to Great Barrier Reef and Mexico

Longhorn cowfish
Lactoria cornuta

Length: 46 cm
Biology: Has two pairs of 'horns' on head and rear body. Fairly rare, solitary; on sand, gravel and seaweed meadows. Feeds on bottom-dwelling invertebrates, which it can expose by blowing a jet of water; 1–100 m.
Distribution: Red Sea to Polynesia

Thornback cowfish
Lactoria fornasini

Length: 15 cm
Biology: Prefers clear lagoons and outreefs; swims close to the seabed, on seaweed meadows, sand and gravel surfaces; male is highly territorial; 1–30 m.
Distribution: East Africa to French Polynesia

Pufferfish
Tetraodontidae

Pufferfish are ponderous swimmers but can manoeuvre themselves with great skill, turn round on the spot or swim backwards. They eat many different plant and animal species; their powerful, beak-like mouths can crack open even hard-shelled prey. They can blow themselves up like a balloon by taking in water; this frightens predators, and makes the puffer too big to fit into the predator's mouth. They also have a bitter taste.

A deadly ball: The primary defence of pufferfish is that they are highly poisonous. Their tissues contain tetrodotoxin, one of the deadliest poisons in nature. It causes paralysis of the muscles – including the breathing muscles, which can lead to asphyxiation. Even sharks will spit out unharmed a pufferfish they have caught if they taste that their prey is poisonous. In certain specialized restaurants in Japan, licensed fugu chefs prepare the pufferfish so that it causes only minor, deliberate poisoning. Elsewhere, however, preparing the fish without proper knowledge has led to many fatal cases of poisoning.

Map puffer
Arothron mappa

Length: 60 cm
Biology: The map puffer has an unmistakable 'maze' pattern that radiates out from its eyes. It is a solitary species but not timid. Can be seen both in lagoons and on outreefs. It feeds on sponges, sea squirts, snails and algae; 4–40 m.
Distribution: East Africa, Maldives to Samoa

Star puffer
Arothron stellatus

Length: 100 cm
Biology: The largest species in the family. The star puffer is seen relatively frequently; it is solitary and feeds on sea urchins, starfish, crustaceans, coral, algae etc. It likes to rest on a sandy seabed, but it is also not unusual to see it several metres away from the reef, swimming at a leisurely pace through open water; 2–52 m.
Distribution: Red Sea to French Polynesia

Masked puffer
Arothron diadematus

Length: 30 cm
Biology: This solitary species is endemic to and common in the Red Sea. It often rests on the seabed, and can also be seen on night dives. During the breeding season it often moves around in fairly large groups; 3–25 m.
Distribution: Red Sea

Blackspotted puffer
Arothron nigropunctatus

Length: 30 cm
Biology: Cream, grey, blue-grey, green-grey, brownish, sometimes yellow, but always with black spots. Feeds on coral, sea squirts and sponges; 1–35 m.
Distribution: East Africa, Maldives to Line Islands and Cook Islands

Valentin's sharpnose puffer
Canthigaster valentini

Length: 10 cm
Biology: Males have a territory with up to 7 females, all of which lay their eggs in bush algae. The eggs are poisonous, and the larvae hatch after 3–5 days; 1–55 m.
Distribution: Gulf of Aden, Maldives to French Polynesia

Papuan toby
Canthigaster papua

Length: 10 cm
Biology: Coral-rich lagoons and outreefs. Feeds on thread and crusting algae, coral and invertebrates; 1–36 m.
Distribution: Indonesia, Papau New Guinea to Palau. Very similar species *C. solandri* from East Africa and Maldives to Polynesia.

Porcupine fish
Diodontidae

Shark v. porcupine fish: A battle with a predictable outcome? Perhaps. But this juicy morsel has stuck in the throat of many a predator. When threatened, porcupine fish swallow water and blow themselves up like a balloon so they are up to four times their normal size. They then get stuck in the predator's throat. Even large sharks and groupers can choke on a porcupine fish. Do not handle these docile fish to induce them to 'blow up' as the stress and the handling may be life-threatening to the fish.

A spiked mace: The spines of porcupine fish make them easy to distinguish from the very similar pufferfish. Some porcupines have fixed spines, others can raise and lower them. When blown up and with their spines sticking out, these 'spiked maces' are an impregnable stronghold for most predators.

Like the pufferfish, their closest relative, porcupines have a beak-shaped mouth. It can bite with great force and crack open hard-shelled prey such as molluscs, snails, sea urchins or hermit crabs. Porcupine fish have strikingly large eyes and tend to be nocturnal. During the day, most of them rest in caves or crevices, or underneath ledges.

Balloonfish
Diodon holocanthus

Length: 50 cm
Biology: Rests in cracks or under ledges during the day, feeds at night on hard-shelled invertebrates; 5–90 m.
Distribution: Red Sea to French Polynesia

Spot-fin porcupine fish
Diodon hystrix

Length: 80 cm
Biology: Rests during the day, usually under ledges or in caves, less frequently swimming in open sea near the reef; 2–50 m.
Distribution: Circumtropical

Orbicular burrfish
Cyclichthys orbicularis

Length: 15 cm
Biology: In sheltered reefs, hides during the day. Hunts at night for prawns, molluscs and worms; 2–20 m.
Distribution: Red Sea to south Japan and north Australia

Reptiles and
Marine Mammals

Sea turtles
Testudines

Sea turtles are able to cover vast distances across the oceans, and have been shown to travel more than 11,000 kilometres. Like migratory birds, they use the earth's magnetic field to guide them. Mating takes place at sea, and the females crawl on to land to lay their eggs, usually returning to their own place of birth.

Green sea turtle
Chelonia mydas

Length: 153 cm
Biology: Comes to land roughly every 2–3 years to lay its eggs. The incubation period usually lasts between 45 and 60 days. The sex of the offspring is determined by the temperature of the nest: above 30 degrees only females develop, below 30 degrees mainly males. Sea turtles (7 species) feed on seaweed, jellyfish, sponges and soft coral, among other food sources. They have to come up to the surface to breathe.
Distribution: All tropical and subtropical seas

Sea snakes
Elapidae

Sea snakes were formerly land-dwellers and have lungs, so they have to come up to the surface to breathe. Even so, they are excellent divers, some diving down as far as 100 metres, although most stay in shallower waters. They can often be seen in cracks and crevices on the reef, busily searching for small prey, mainly fish.

Black & white sea krait
Laticauda colubrina

Length: 150 cm (larger in Fiji)
Biology: This is the species most often seen by divers in its distribution area. It belongs to the small group of flat-tail sea snakes, which – unlike most other species – go on land to rest, mate and lay their eggs. Feeds mainly on moray eels. Is highly poisonous but normally non-aggressive to humans.
Distribution: Sri Lanka and Eastern India to Tonga

Dugongs
Dugong dugon

Grazing: Their name says it all: 'sea cows' graze on seaweed meadows. This method of nutrition makes the dugong unique: it is the world's only plant-eating mammal that lives exclusively in the sea. Its close relatives, the manatees, from the south-eastern United States, all live in fresh water.

Dugong
Dugong dugon

Length: Up to 350 cm
Biology: Lives in wide, shallow coves with seagrass meadows. Grows to at least 400 kg and up to a maximum of 900 kg, and can live for 70 years. A single calf is born after a gestation period of 13–15 months, and a strong and very close bond is formed between mother and calf. The young dugong feeds from its mother for up to 18 months.
Distribution: Red Sea to Vanuatu, but nowadays only sporadically

Dolphins
Delphinidae

Dolphins are highly developed, intelligent and social marine mammals. Their streamlined shape makes them fast, skilled swimmers and good divers. They navigate and find their prey using ultrasonic location, and they communicate by means of a complex sonar language of clicks and whistles.

Indo-Pacific bottlenose dolphin
Tursiops aduncus

Length: 260 cm
Biology: Biologists are still uncertain whether the greater and lesser bottlenose dolphins are two different species or just sub-species. The lesser bottlenose, however, lives mainly in coastal waters, and tends to stay within its 300 km^2 territory. Present on many reefs in the Red Sea and the Maldives, it is a regular sight.
Distribution: Red Sea to Australia and Japan

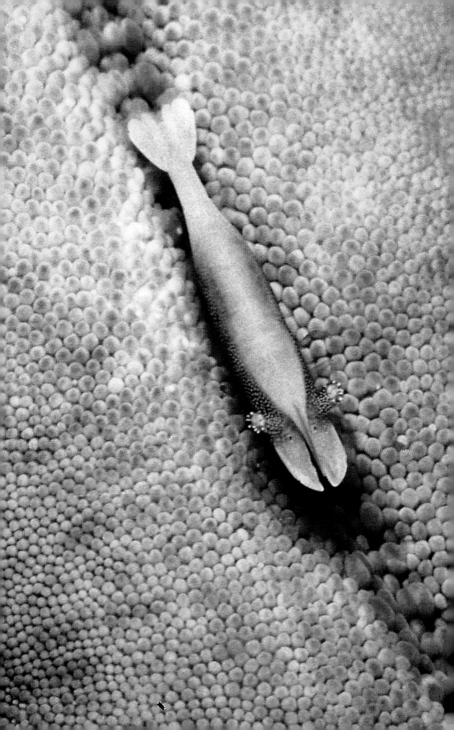

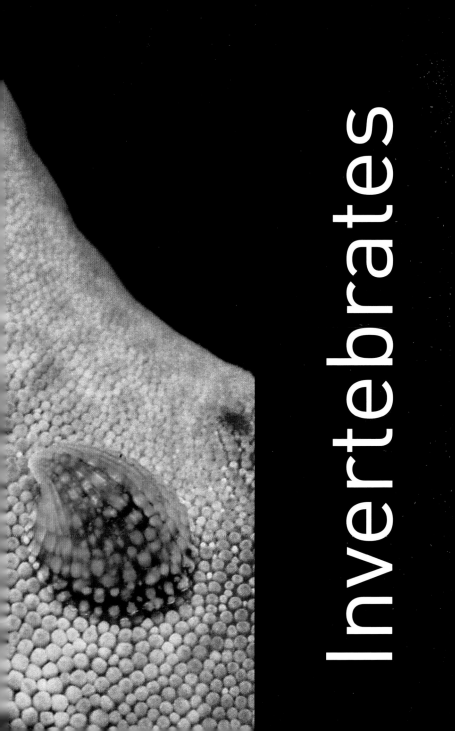

Invertebrates

Sponges
Porifera

Pumping station: Around 8,000 species of sponges have already been recorded, but marine biologists are constantly discovering new ones, and estimate that there are about 25,000 species in total. Sponges feed on minute particles by taking in the water around them through tiny pores on their surface, pumping it through a network of channels and retaining the food particles, and then pumping out the filtered water through large outlet openings. A sponge the size of a football can process about 3,000 litres of water every day, filtering out up to 99% of the bacteria, single-celled algae and organic particles held in it.

A seabed chemist's shop: Sponges possess a huge variety of chemical antigens that protect them from predators and prevent them from becoming overgrown. This chemical arsenal is a goldmine for pharmaceutical researchers because some of these substances can be used in medicine. A number of drugs have already been developed from sponges, including treatments for virus infections and cancer.

Red Sea sponge
Negombata corticata

Length: 70 cm
Biology: Branched like fingers or antlers. At the slightest injury or pressure, this species exudes a red liquid, which is highly toxic to fish and causes the fish to move away immediately. The sponge is eaten mainly by the pyjama slug (*see* page 192) which uses the toxin from the sponge (latrunculin) for its own defence.
Distribution: Red Sea, Indian Ocean

Barrel sponge
Xestospongia testudinaria

Length: 150 cm, diameter up to 50 cm
Biology: Varies from barrel- to vase-shaped. On the outside it has deep, irregular vertical corrugations that increase the surface area for the countless minute inlet openings. The largest tropical sponge, it is frequently colonized by other animals, such as feather stars, small sea cucumbers (*Synaptula* sp.) or the pink hairy squat (*Lauriea siagiani*).
Distribution: Indonesia, New Guinea to the Philippines

Fire coral
Milleporidae

Because of their sturdy limestone skeleton, fire corals are often thought to be stone corals. In fact, like the sea ferns, they belong to the hydrozoa. Just like reef-building stone corals they live in symbiosis with single-celled algae, and form part of the reef structure with their limestone framework. There are net, plate and encrusted species.

Net fire coral
Millepora dichotoma

Height: 60 cm
Biology: Surface covered with minute holes, in each of which there is a polyp (millepora means 'thousand pores'). Because of its light-dependent algae (zooxanthellae) it colonizes the higher parts of the reef. Widespread in some areas on reef edges and well-lit slopes. Caution: contact causes a burning sensation, inflammation and welts.
Distribution: Red Sea to Samoa

Sea ferns
Plumulariidae

Sea ferns are found in all oceans in a variety
of species, some with powerful stings.
Typical growth forms are feather, bush and
tree shapes. Some are very delicate and lacy
with few branches, others are much sturdier
and heavily branched. The colonies can range
in size from a few centimetres to species that
are one metre in height.

Stinging hydroid
Macrorhynchia philippina

Height: 30 cm
Biology: Colonizes hard ground,
usually in places with a good
current flow. Probably migrated
to the Mediterranean via the Suez
Canal. The colonies look delicate
but in fact are very robust, and are
anchored in the ground by root-like
runners. Can sting if touched, and
may trigger an allergic reaction.
Distribution: Worldwide in
tropical seas

Jellyfish
Scyphozoa

Jellyfish are present in every ocean, from the tropics to the Arctic, from the surface to the lowest depths. The approximately 200–250 species have an umbrella diameter ranging from a few centimetres to over 2 m.

Settlers and nomads: The life cycle of most species has an alternation of generations. The small polyp stage, which remains fixed on the seabed, changes into the freely swimming medusa stage, which roams across the oceans and with which we are familiar. The next generation is then the polyp stage, and the cycle begins once again.

Glutton: Many species live only for a year, some only a few months. During this time they eat a lot. The common or moon jellyfish consumes up to 20,000 plankton every day, and larger species correspondingly more. In this way even the largest species grow to their full size in a matter of months.

Slimming diet: Many jellyfish go through long periods of starvation when they lose huge amounts of weight. Animals with an umbrella diameter of 40 cm can shrink down to the size of a one-euro coin. When sufficient food is available, they quickly grow back to their old size.

Crown jellyfish
Cephea cephea

Diameter: 15 cm
Biology: Pelagic species, also brought by currents close to the shore. Sting is very weak, often unnoticed.
Distribution: Red Sea to Polynesia

Common or moon jellyfish
Aurelia aurita

Diameter: Max. 50 cm
Biology: Locally common, can form huge swarms. Most have very weak stings.
Distribution: Several species worldwide; *A. maldivensis* (25 cm): Red Sea, Indian Ocean

Upside-down jellyfish
Cassiopea andromeda

Diameter: 12 cm
Biology: In shallow waters up to 15 m. Lies on its 'back' to give maximum sunlight to its zooxanthellae.
Distribution: Red Sea to Western Pacific

Soft corals
Alcyonaria

Pincushion: Soft corals have numerous limestone nodules embedded in their fleshy tissues. Most of these nodules are very small, but some can be up to 1 cm long, as in the *Dendronephthya* species. These species shrink when they lose water, when the nodules protrude clearly.

A chemical cudgel: In addition, soft corals contain many chemical antigens. Most species are highly toxic to fish, or are at the very least protected by the deterrent action of their anti-predator substances.

Adaptation: Very few predators are immune to such chemical weapons. Some butterfly fish occasionally nibble off polyps of soft coral, while sea turtles can eat entire colonies. Some sea slugs, too, are specialist feeders on specific soft corals. Many species live in symbiosis with photosynthesizing zooxanthellae, whose products contribute substantially to the coral's nutrition. The brightly-coloured species have no symbiotic algae and feed on plankton.

Klunzinger's soft coral
Dendronephthya klunzingeri

Size: 100 cm
Biology: Forms magnificent growths in some areas. Mostly pink to purplish-red; colour is not an indication of species, which can only be established with certainty from the nodules. Often shrinks during the day following water loss; in many areas catches plankton mainly at night.
Distribution: Red Sea to Western Pacific

Vibrant soft coral
Dendronephthya hemprichi

Size: 70 cm
Biology: Tree-like, but branches are mostly in two dimensions only. Orange or pink. Only a few years ago it was discovered that this species feeds almost exclusively on minute plankton algae. The effectiveness of this plant food source is demonstrated by young specimens in particular, which can achieve growth rates of more than 8% per day.
Distribution: Red Sea to Western Pacific

Lobate leather coral
Lobophytum sp.

Size: 70 cm (across)
Biology: Nutrition augmented by the photosynthesis of zooxanthellae, so lives in well-lit places.
Distribution: Red Sea to Western Pacific

Common toadstool coral
Sarcophyton trocheliophorum

Size: 80 cm (across)
Biology: Nutrition augmented by the photosynthesis of zooxanthellae, so lives in well-lit places.
Distribution: Red Sea to Western Pacific

Finger leather coral
Sinularia leptoclados

Size: 30 cm (per clump)
Biology: Has densely-packed calcium sclerites, which form a dense adhesive mass at the base of the colony. Can form columns several metres high, thus forming part of the reef structure.
Distribution: Red Sea to Western Pacific

Pulsating xenid
Heteroxenia fuscescens

Height: 16 cm
Biology: Long-stemmed polyps cluster on a compact stem. The polyps open and close their rings of tentacles in a characteristic pumping movement. Has zooxanthellae.
Distribution: Red Sea to Indian Ocean

Horn corals
Gorgonacea

Horn corals have a supporting skeleton that is firm but flexible, made up of limestone nodules bonded together, in most cases with a horn-like substance, gorgonin, which forms a fibrous bond. This flexible core is surrounded by a soft bark in which the polyps are embedded.

Many mouths: The surface is densely covered with polyps – many thousands, in the case of large fan colonies. When open, they form a giant, fine-meshed net, which catches plankton carried in by the current. The polyps act like a single organism with many mouths. It is not essential for an individual polyp to feed, as long as the adjacent polyps do so, which then share the nutrition obtained.

In order to catch plankton more effectively, fan gorgonians grow at right angles to the current. All species that do not have zooxanthellae live by catching plankton, and are often vividly coloured. There are also species with zooxanthellae, which grow in shallow waters with good light and are more muted in colour.

Knotted fan
Melithaea ochracea

Size: 100 cm
Biology: Lives on steep reef slopes, catches microplankton. Colour variable but mainly pink, orange-red or purple.
Distribution: Indian Ocean, Western Pacific

Giant sea fan
Annella mollis

Size: 200 cm
Biology: Pale cream in the Red Sea, elsewhere yellowish, or orange-red. Prefers exposed, steep reef slopes.
Distribution: Red Sea to Western Pacific

Red cluster whip
Ellisella juncea

Size: 60 cm
Biology: Likes an exposed position with a strong current. Like all colourful gorgonians, does not have zooxanthellae.
Distribution: Red Sea to Western Pacific

Sea feathers
Pennatulacea

Sea feathers colonize sandy and muddy surfaces. They have a fleshy stem and a powerful burrowing foot, with which they anchor themselves deep in the soft ground. They generally stay in one location, but if necessary they can move away by alternately spreading and elongating the foot in order to find a better position.

Common sea feather
Pteroides sp.

Length: Up to 60 cm
Biology: Sea feathers are nocturnal and catch zooplankton. During the day, they usually bury themselves completely in the sediment. The colony is able to contract and open out by expelling and taking in water respectively. Small commensal crustaceans often live among the polyps, where they find food and shelter.
Distribution: Red Sea to Western Pacific

Crust anemones
Zoantharia

Most species of crust anemone form colonies. The polyps measure barely 1 cm or 2 cm across, but they can build colonies of more than a thousand individuals, forming huge cushions that cover large areas. Some species (*Palythoa*) are known to contain the highly poisonous palytoxin.

Button polyp
Protopalythoa sp.

Size: 1 cm (diameter of polyp)
Biology: Crust anemones are very difficult to identify, so most of them are known only by their generic name. Many have a rough feel because they incorporate silicon-containing particles or grains of sand in their tissues. Many have symbiotic algae, and are brownish or greenish in colour accordingly.
Distribution: Indian and Pacific Oceans

Tube-dwelling anemones
Ceriantharia

The group contains about 50 species and lives on sandy ground in all seas, from shallow water to deep oceans. Tube-dwelling anemones have a worm-like foot with a pointed base for burrowing in the sand. They make a parchment-like tube from mucus and sand into which they retract when threatened. They use their tentacles to catch zooplankton.

Giant tube anemone
Cerianthus cf. filiformis

Size: 30 cm
Biology: Like all species, it has short mouth tentacles, which push its prey into its throat, surrounded by long, sticky tentacles for catching. As in other species, the colour of the long tentacles varies, ranging in this case from white to brown, blue or purple, always with pale-coloured mouth tentacles. Catches mainly plankton at night, possibly small fish also.
Distribution: In large areas of the Indo-Pacific

Disc anemones
Corallimorpharia

Disc anemones are closely related to stone corals, and look like anemones without tentacles, but they have no skeleton. Some species live singly, others can form large carpets measuring several metres across. Worldwide there are roughly 50 species; some have strong stinging capsules and can give a painful sting.

Balloon corallimorph
Amplexidiscus fenestrafer

Width: 45 cm
Biology: Lives on sheltered reefs, sometimes in groups, usually between 10 and 30 m on gravel or dead coral. Its main source of food is the photosynthesis of its symbiotic zooxanthellae, but it also catches zooplankton and possibly small fish by slowly closing its large, doughnut-shaped disc into a ball. Can sting with a painful burn if touched.
Distribution: Indo-Pacific

Sea anemones
Actinaria

Sea anemones look like plants but are cnidarians, and are predatory feeders. They live individually but can also cluster together in dense groups. Most species have long, conspicuous tentacles that contain stinging capsules, but only a few of the roughly 1,000 species are able to give a noticeable sting to a human – and very few a powerful one.

Sea anemones live anchored to rocky or sediment ground, spending most of their lives in the same spot. However, if necessary, they are able to move slowly. If threatened, many species form a ball or withdraw quickly into crevices or into their mud burrows. They use their tentacles to catch minute organisms from the water, but are also able to eat crustaceans and fish.

Fellowship: Many species host zooxanthellae, which provide almost all their nutritional needs. Some are home to various crustaceans and fish. Anemone fish in particular sometimes defend their host resolutely against predators.

Magnificent anemone
Heteractis magnifica

Size: Diameter 100 cm
Biology: Frequently a host for anemone fish, and also for damselfish, shrimps and porcelain crabs; stem usually vividly coloured, e.g. blue, purple, red, nut-brown or white. Has photosynthesizing zooxanthellae, which contribute to its nutrition; also catches zooplankton. Typically in exposed locations; 1–30 m.
Distribution: Red Sea to French Polynesia

Adhesive anemone
Cryptodendron adhaesivum

Size: Diameter 35 cm
Biology: Colour variable: green, brown, olive, sometimes very colourful. The tentacles are small and very sticky. This species withdraws quickly into a rock crevice if disturbed. Rarely colonized by anemone fish (*A. clarkii*, if at all), but often by partner shrimps (*Periclimenes bevicarpalis*).
Distribution: Red Sea to Western Pacific

Stone corals
Scleractinia

Master builders: Stone corals are a vital part of reef structure, and are often appropriately referred to as the master builders of the reefs. The polyps of the hermatypic (reef-building) corals host a layer of single-celled symbiotic algae (zooxanthellae) just under the surface of their bodies. The algae are highly concentrated within the tissues of the polyps, and by their photosynthesis make a major contribution to the feeding and growth of the corals. Polyps and algae live in a close nutrient exchange relationship. The algae pass most of the energy-rich compounds produced during photosynthesis on to their host polyps, and in return they receive from the polyps compounds containing oxygen and phosphorus, together with the carbon dioxide they need for photosynthesis. Tropical seas are low in nutrients, so this close symbiosis provides the most effective recycling of important nutrients and trace elements. The algae are also very important for the coral's formation of limestone.

Yellow scroll coral
Turbinaria mesenterina

Size: Diameter 300 cm
Biology: Striking, sulphur-yellow colonies of convoluted, lettuce-like plates. The upper surfaces have a nubbly appearance because of the cone-shaped polyp calyces. Prefers a sunny location.
Distribution: Red Sea to French Polynesia

Table coral
Acropora clathrata

Size: Diameter to more than 200 cm
Biology: Cantilevered growth pattern; horizontal table-like plates made up of lots of finely-branched twigs, which can form an almost solid plate. There are several very similar species. Lives on sheltered reef slopes, especially under the edge of the reef and on the uppermost reef slope.
Distribution: Red Sea to Polynesia

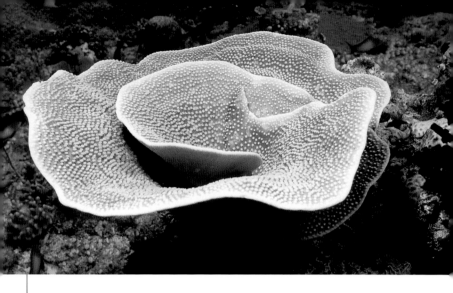

Maze coral
Pachyseris speciosa

Size: 300 cm
Biology: Forms large, funnel-shaped plates with concentric furrows on top, smooth on the underside. Grows on middle and deep reef slopes, 20 m and below. Also grows in encrusted form on steep slopes.
Distribution: Red Sea to French Polynesia

Bubble coral
Plerogyra sinuosa

Size: Diameter 150 cm
Biology: Beige to greyish-green. During the daytime, it is covered with bubbles, which provide the zooxanthellae with the best conditions for photosynthesis. At night, the polyps extend their tentacles to catch plankton.
Distribution: Red Sea to French Polynesia

Staghorn coral
Acropora formosa

Height: 150 cm
Biology: Beige to brownish or bluish; ends usually pale and fast-growing, 2–6 cm per year. Common, and often the dominant species in sheltered lagoon fringing reefs; can cover large areas.
Distribution: Red Sea to French Polynesia

Brain coral
Platygyra daedalea

Size: 200 cm
Biology: Huge colonies with maze-like grooves. Beige to light olive. Often lives on reef tops and upper reef slopes, up to 30 m.
Distribution: Red Sea to French Polynesia

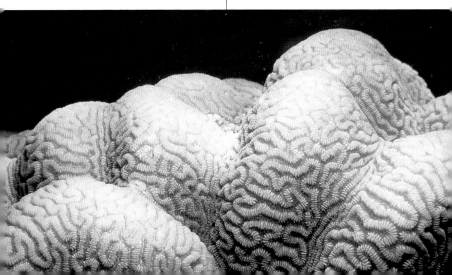

Little thorn corals
Antipathidae

Little thorn corals are also known as black corals, although this normally refers to the large, bush-like colonies. However, it is only the axial skeleton that is black, and this is not visible from the outside in living colonies because it is covered by tissue in which the polyps are embedded.

Black jewels: The horny black skeleton of some large species has been made into jewellery since ancient times. In some areas, whole branches of the bushy types are also sold as souvenirs. As a result, they are heavily fished in many places and stocks have been badly depleted. In addition, black coral used to be sold as a medicine or lucky charm against illness in Europe, and still is in Asia. This is the origin of its scientific name (*Antipathes* means 'against illness').

The species most commonly seen by divers in the Indo-Pacific are those illustrated here, as well as *Cirrhipathes anguina*. This is very similar to *Cirrhipathes spiralis* but is smaller – less than 100 cm – and less regular.

Spiral coral
Cirrhipathes spiralis

Size: 250 cm
Biology: As in the branching black coral, closer inspection reveals the numerous tiny thorns and hooks on the surface, which give the little thorn corals their name. Lives in a location with a strong current, usually below 10 m. The polyps catch plankton that are driven past by the current.
Distribution: Red Sea to Western Pacific

Branching black coral
Antipathes dichotoma

Size: 300 cm
Biology: Prefers steep reef slopes with strong currents; usually below 30 m, but in some places in far shallower water. Grows very slowly: a large colony with a base stem of arm thickness is many decades old. Often colonized by other plankton-feeders such as feather stars, brittle stars and winged oysters. A favourite residence also of longnose hawkfish.
Distribution: Red Sea to French Polynesia

Bristleworms
Polychaeta

There are around 10,000 known species of brittleworm, almost all of which live in the sea. They live in plankton, buried in sand or mud, and also in crevices or moving around freely in rock and coral reefs. There are two distinct groups.

On patrol: Mobile species are mainly predatory feeders and are mostly nocturnal. They eat other worms, crustaceans, non-mobile creatures and detritus.

In a few species the bristles are used for defence. They are positioned in dense clumps and can easily penetrate human skin, where they break off; their poison causes a painful burning sensation.

Sedentary: Other species have given up their mobile lifestyle for a more sedentary one. They specialize in catching plankton, and have developed a crown of tentacles for that purpose; this is normally all that is visible of the worm. The rest of the body is hidden inside a tube it has made and which it will never leave. The *Sabellidae* family lives in tubes that have a rubbery or parchment texture; *Serpulidae* live in limestone tubes.

Christmas tree worm
Spirobranchus giganteus

Size: Diameter 1.5 cm (crown)
Biology: Embedded in living coral, often in groups. The crown is made up of two spiral rings of tentacles; colour very variable: white, yellow, orange, blue, dark purple, blackish, sometimes also spotted. Plankton feeder. Very timid, retracts instantly in response to any suspicious shadow or wave movement.
Distribution: circumtropical

Peacock bristleworm
Chloea flava

Length: 10 cm
Biology: Usually on sand or gravel; regularly seen in coastal areas. Scavenger and predator, is able to swim across the seabed. Broad body with dense tufts of long yellow bristles. Caution: the bristles will cause a burning pain if touched.
Distribution: Red Sea to Western Pacific

Flatworms
Platyhelminthes

Gliders: Most marine flatworms grow to several centimetres in length, some to more than 10 cm. Several hundred species are already known, but marine biologists regularly discover new ones. Flatworms are the masters of a fast, fluent gliding motion over the seabed, adjusting to any unevenness in the ground. Some of the larger species are able to swim using wave-like movements, but only for short distances.

A keen nose: They find their way primarily by scent when searching for food or a mate. To do this, they stretch up their 'heads' at intervals in order to gauge the direction of a scent more accurately.

Special diet: Most species are predators and prefer to feed on non-mobile invertebrates. Many individual species, though, have specialized dietary requirements, and their menu includes sponges, bryozoans and sea squirts, for example. Flatworms are well protected against predators by toxins stored in their bodies, and the vivid patterns on many species are probably intended as a warning sign.

Gold-dotted flatworm
Thysanozoon nigropapillosum

Length: 5 cm
Biology: Relatively common. This species is often seen swimming by means of wave-like movements
Distribution: Red Sea, many very similar species in the Indo-Pacific

Glorious flatworm
Pseudobiceros gloriosus

Length: 9 cm
Biology: Many very similar species with marginal edges in different colour combinations. Is able to swim; mainly nocturnal.
Distribution: Red Sea to Hawaii

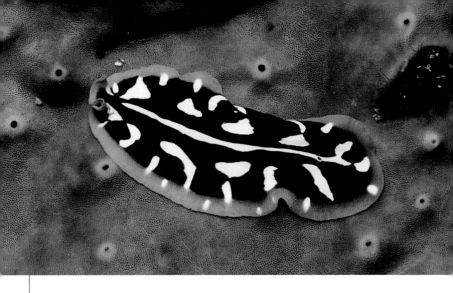

Divided flatworm
Pseudoceros dimidiatus

Length: 4 cm
Biology: Very little is known about some flatworm species, including this magnificent one.
Distribution: Maldives, Indian Ocean, Indonesia, Fiji, Palau

Fuchsia flatworm
Pseudoceros cf. ferugineus

Length: 5 cm
Biology: Background colour rusty red to scarlet, with a dense sprinkling of small white spots. Feeds on colony-forming sea squirts, active by both day and night.
Distribution: Red Sea to Polynesia

Bedford's flatworm
Pseudobiceros bedfordi

Length: 10 cm
Biology: A large, eye-catching species in a variety of strong, intense colourings. Can glide across the seabed very quickly, and is an elegant swimmer. Its diet includes sea squirts.
Distribution: Red Sea to Western Pacific

Orsak's flatworm
Maiazoon orsaki

Length: 6 cm
Biology: Cream-coloured with a brown ruffled edge tipped with black. Its small eyespot is visible in the middle of its head. The photo shows it on a colony of sea squirts, one of its food sources.
Distribution: Indo-Pacific

Prosobranch snails
Prosobranchia

Snails are the largest group of molluscs, with more than 110,000 species. Most are shelled snails, i.e. they have a protective shell.

Grater: A typical feature of snails is their highly developed rasping tongue (radula). This carries many minute teeth, enabling the snail to graze algae from surfaces. In doing this they also eat numerous invertebrates, and some are able to use a drilling action to make circular holes in the shells of other snails or molluscs. Some, like the cone snail, have highly modified tongues.

Poison arrows: All cone snails are active hunters able to catch even agile fish. That proverbially slow snails are able to do this is a remarkable natural development. Cone snails hunt with poison arrows, and their venom is one of the most powerful known: some types can kill a person very quickly. However, humans are only in danger if they collect or handle them. For safety's sake, cone snails should never be touched.

Triton's trumpet
Charonia tritonis

Length: 50 cm
Biology: A nocturnal predator, hunts large starfish, including crown-of-thorns starfish. Uses sulphuric acid to dissolve the shells of sea urchins.
Distribution: Red Sea to Polynesia; Mediterranean

Umbilical ovula
Calpurnus verrucosus

Length: 4.5 cm
Biology: Feeds mainly on *Sarcophyton* and *Lobophyton* soft corals (page 166), also on sponges.
Distribution: Red Sea to Fiji

Textile cone shell
Conus textile

Length: 15 cm
Biology: Nocturnal, feeds on snails and cone snails, worms and fish. Extremely dangerous. Lives up to 9 years.
Distribution: Red Sea to French Polynesia

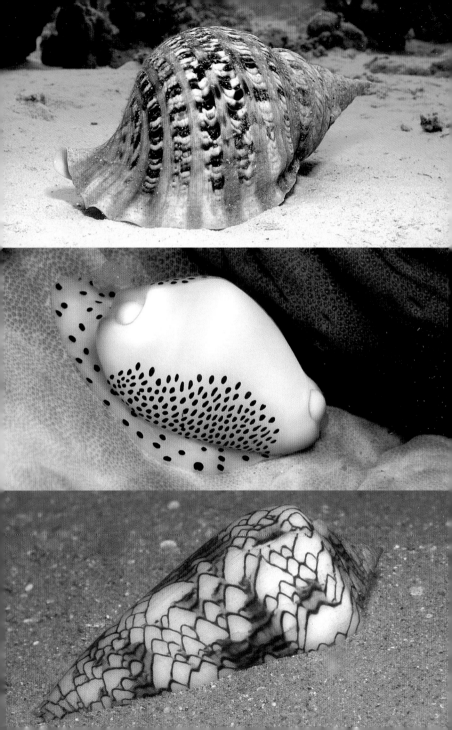

Sea slugs
Nudibranchia

Sea slugs grow very quickly. Most species live only a few months, and the few that live as long as a year are almost Methuselahs. During their short lives some species grow to between 1 cm and 10 cm; few grow larger than this. Sea slugs have an ingenious defence system, and are fond of eating poisonous prey. These two facts are connected: many non-mobile animals such as sponges, cnidarians and sea squirts are protected against predators by toxins in their tissues. Most sea slug species, however, have developed their feeding habits to specialize in eating these non-mobile creatures.

Poison reservoir: They are immune to the poison of their prey, and even store the venomous substances in their own tissues, thus themselves becoming poisonous and therefore protected against predators. Shag-rug snails eat cnidarians and store the latter's poison capsules in their own dorsal appendages for their own protection. Some also take over the symbiotic algae (zooxanthellae) of their prey.

Purple nudibranch
Nembrotha purpureolineolata

Length: 6 cm
Biology: Like other *Nembrotha* slugs this is a surprisingly fast, agile creature.
Distribution: East Africa to Japan and Western Australia

Pyjama nudibranch
Chromodoris quadricolor

Length: 4.5 cm
Biology: One of the Red Sea's commonest and most familiar species. Feeds on the Red Sea sponge (page 160).
Distribution: Red Sea to Tanzania

Tryon's nudibranch
Risbecia tryoni

Length: 10 cm
Biology: Frequently prowls around in pairs in single file, the slug at the back using its head to maintain contact with the one at the front.
Distribution: East Africa to French Polynesia

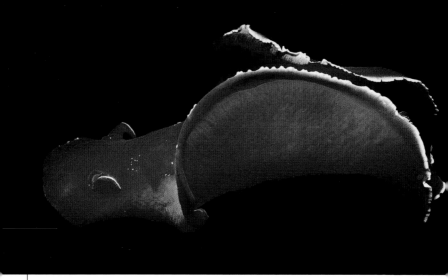

Spanish dancer
Hexabranchus sanguineus

Length: Up to 50 cm
Biology: One of the largest species, and can swim in spectacular fashion using elegant wave-like movements. Scarlet in the Red Sea (*see* photo), mostly 'only' 30 cm long. Orange or yellow in other places.
Distribution: Red Sea to French Polynesia

Kune's chromodoris
Chromodoris kuniei

Length: 5 cm
Biology: Common, feeds on sponges. There are at least two very similar species in the Indo-Pacific that differ in their colour patterning (*C. geminus* and *C. tritos*).
Distribution: Indonesia to Australia, Philippines and Marshall Islands

Eyespot nudibranch
Phyllidia ocellata

Length: 6 cm
Biology: A common species with many colour variants; *P. undula* (Red Sea) has black-and-white, wave-like stripes, and may itself be only a variant. Feeds on sponges.
Distribution: (Red Sea), Indian Ocean to Western Pacific

Serpent pteraeolidia
Pteraeolidia ianthina

Length: 10 cm
Biology: Colour variable: green, blue or purple, depending on the algae in its tissues. Eats cnidarians such as sea fern and leather coral, adopting their stinging capsules and symbiotic algae.
Distribution: Red Sea to French Polynesia

Bivalves
Bivalvia

Like snails and cephalopods, bivalves belong to the mollusc group (Mollusca). Most bivalves are active filter feeders. They take in water through a breathing aperture and eject it through an outlet opening, at the same time filtering out plankton as the water passes over the gills. Some species, such as the giant clam, have symbiotic algae, which supply them with additional nutrients from photosynthesis.

Most species burrow in the sand, while others fasten themselves to hard surfaces by means of byssal threads. Some bore into rock or coral branches. Fileshell mussels can swim short distances when threatened, using a 'skipping' motion by clapping the two parts of their shell together.

Some molluscs produce pearls by covering an introduced irritant, such as a grain of sand, with layers of mother of pearl. Some species have rows of simple eyes on the edge of the outer shell, and also sensory cells that react to pressure waves: the thorny oyster, for example, will snap its shell closed instantly if a diver approaches carelessly.

Squamose giant clam
Tridacna squamosa

Length: 40 cm
Biology: A thick, wavy shell with deeply convoluted, widely separated scales. The outer shell is usually greyish-blue, green or brownish. Mostly more or less firmly embedded in crevices, or grown into coral blocks. Feeds mainly on the photosynthesis products made by its zooxanthellae. Closes its shell relatively slowly when disturbed.
Distribution: Red Sea to Samoa

Orange-mouth thorny oyster
Spondylus varius

Length: 25 cm
Biology: Shell is always covered with algae, sponges and other colonizers. Outer shell very colourful and variable: yellow, orange, red, blue and lilac markings, and rows of small eyes on the upper and lower edges. Closes its shell immediately and very quickly at the slightest disturbance.
Distribution: Red Sea to the Marshall Islands

Octopuses
Octopodidae

All members of the octopus family are typical bottom-dwellers, but octopuses are able to swim, although they rarely do so. They swim using a jet-propulsion method, expelling water through their movable breathing siphon. The octopus can change colour within a fraction of a second to camouflage itself against its background.

Day octopus
Octopus cyanea

Size: 100 cm
Biology: The most common species seen by divers on Indo-Pacific coral reefs. Active by day also. Lives in lagoons and outreefs, from the shallows down to more than 25 m. Uses small caves or crevices as a burrow, frequently reducing the size of the entrance with molluscs and stones. Eats mainly prawns, sometimes also molluscs and fish.
Distribution: Red Sea to Polynesia

Cuttlefish
Sepiidae

Cuttlefish can change instantly to a variety
of different colour patterns. They have eight
arms, plus two longer tentacles covered with
suckers, which they throw out far in front of
them to catch their prey. Although cuttlefish
live on the seabed, they often swim or hover
slightly above the ground.

Pharaoh cuttlefish
Sepia pharaonis

Size: 40 cm (body)
Biology: Can change not only its
colour but also the structure of its
skin, using muscle contractions to
form ragged protuberances and
flaps on its normally smooth skin.
When disturbed, and also during
the breeding season, it has distinct
horizontal stripes. Frequently
swims at night in shallow water,
feeds on crustaceans and fish;
0.3–110 m.
Distribution: Red Sea to Japan

Crustaceans
Crustacea

Knights of the sea: About 45,000 species of crustaceans have been recorded, but there could be many more, since new ones are constantly being discovered. Crustaceans have been wearing suits of armour for more than 500 million years. With many developments and variations, the basic principle is still the same: a movable exoskeleton that covers the animal completely. Despite their armour, crustaceans are highly mobile and agile, as their protection is made of chitin, which is both hard and lightweight.

New armour: An exoskeleton has a major drawback, however: it does not get bigger as its wearer grows. It has to be replaced at intervals when a growth spurt is due to take place. This is when crustaceans moult. The new armour is formed underneath the old one before the latter is shed. Once the creature has worked its way out of the old shell, which is now too small, it can make a sudden growth spurt because the new shell is still soft and flexible. Some species can grow up to 30 per cent in length at each moult.

Harlequin shrimp
Hymenocera elegans

Length: 5 cm
Biology: Usually lives in a pair with a territory, a permanent bond that can last for years. The bond is ensured by a pheromone produced by the female. They cooperate to turn starfish upside down, and then they eat its feet and viscera.
Distribution: Red Sea to Indonesia

Banded coral shrimp
Stenopus hispidus

Length: 5 cm
Biology: Usually lives in crevices, sometimes in pairs; males are smaller than females. They maintain cleaning stations, enticing client fish to their shelters by waving their antennae. Cleaning symbiosis benefits both parties: the fish have their skin parasites removed and the shrimps get a meal.
Distribution: Circumtropical

Painted spiny lobster
Panulirus versicolor

Length: 40 cm
Biology: Spend the day in crevices, often with their long antennae protruding. Sociable, frequently in small groups. Prowl the reef at night, eating molluscs, starfish, worms and dead fish; 1 to at least 50 m.
Distribution: Red Sea to French Polynesia

Clam digger
Scyllarides tridacnophaga

Length: 35 cm
Biology: Nocturnal. Able to open giant clams and dig out prey from soft ground using its plate-like antennae. When threatened, moves quickly away backwards by collapsing its tail sections; 1–122 m.
Distribution: Red Sea to Thailand

Anemone hermit crab
Dardanus pedunculatus

Length: 10 cm
Biology: Nocturnal, predatory omnivore. Almost always lives in symbiosis with an anemone, which it takes with it when moving to a new housing.
Distribution: East Africa, Maldives to French Polynesia

Porcelain anemone crab
Neopetrolisthes oshima

Length: 2.5 cm
Biology: Almost invariably lives in pairs on sea anemones. Feeds by filtration, waving around its third pair of gnathopods, which have long, fine bristles.
Distribution: Indo- and Western Pacific

Red reef crab
Carpilius convexus

Length: 9 cm
Biology: Colour variable: uniform orange-red to reddish-brown, or marbled. Lives on reef tops and slopes. Feeds at night on snails and sea urchins, opens shells with its powerful claws.
Distribution: Red Sea to French Polynesia

Harlequin crab
Lissocarcinus orbicularis

Length: 4 cm
Biology: Colour variable: dark brown to orange pattern on a white background, or vice versa. Often on sea cucumbers, on which they live commensally; timid, often remains on underside of cucumber during the day.
Distribution: Red Sea to Fiji

Peacock mantis shrimp
Odontodactylus scyllarus

Length: 18 cm
Biology: Raptorial legs with club-like swelling to break up hard-shelled prey. Lives in a U-shaped tube, into which it withdraws if disturbed, but can also be curious and bold.
Distribution: East Africa, Maldives to Samoa

Common mantis shrimp
Pseudosquilla ciliata

Length: 10 cm
Biology: Raptorial legs with long spines for impaling its prey. Black, green, yellow, white, sometimes patterned. Can adapt its colour to a new environment within months.
Distribution: circumtropical apart from the Eastern Pacific

Feather stars
Crinoidea

Feather stars have very flexible arms and are often brightly coloured. They are able to move and hold themselves in position by the claw-like cilia on their undersides. Some hide in crevices during the day and climb up at night to exposed positions on the reef, where they stretch out their arms to catch plankton in the current.

Variable bushy feather star
Comanthina schlegelii

Height: 20 cm
Biology: Very common. Colour very variable: sometimes a uniform colour, sometimes arms and pinna are a different colour. Has up to 130 closely-packed arms. Can be seen in the daytime also, on exposed locations with strong currents. It often holds itself in position not only with its cilia but also with its lower, and often shorter, arms.
Distribution: Maldives to Western Pacific

Brittle stars
Ophiuroidea

With 2,000 species, the brittle stars are the largest group of the echinoderm genus, which also includes feather stars, starfish, sea urchins and sea cucumbers. They hide in crevices, under stones or in soft ground during the day, and emerge at night, when they graze detritus from the ground or catch plankton from the water.

Long-spined brittle star
Ophiotrix savignyi

Length: 15 cm
Biology: Their flexible arms make brittle stars highly mobile and relatively fast: they are the sprinters of their genus. They crawl by bending and stretching their arms forwards. The arms are easily broken off; if a predator grabs one of them, it can snap off at any point, allowing the brittle star to escape.
Distribution: Red Sea to New Caledonia

Starfish
Asteroidea

Around 1,600 species are known, varying in diameter from less than 1 cm to more than 100 cm. Most have five arms but some species have more. They move by means of the numerous small feet – there can be several hundred to over a thousand – on the underside of their bodies; the arms themselves hardly move at all.

Invertible stomach: Many species are predators, but they also eat carrion. Their prey include a wide range of invertebrates including sponges, crustaceans, snails, molluscs, bryozoa, sea squirts, and also other starfish. Many species are not choosy and will eat whatever they find and are able to overpower. Starfish do not have a mouth: they feed by inverting their many-folded stomachs over their prey. If the prey is too large, it is pre-digested outside the starfish's body, and then eaten in liquefied form.

Many species are able to fully regenerate missing arms. Some, especially the *Linckia* species, reproduce asexually by breaking off one of their own arms, which will eventually grow into a complete starfish.

Blue star
Linckia laevigata

Length: 40 cm
Biology: Can break off one of its own arms, which will then grow into a complete animal.
Distribution: East Africa, Indo-Pacific to Hawaii

Granulated sea star
Choriaster granulatus

Length: 25 cm
Biology: Colour variable: white, cream, orange to red. Lives on hard surfaces and living coral, feeds on detritus and small invertebrates.
Distribution: Red Sea to Fiji

Crown-of-thorns starfish
Acanthaster planci

Length: 50 cm
Biology: Feeds on the polyps of stone coral. When present in large numbers, can seriously damage large areas of reef. Caution: spines are poisonous.
Distribution: Red Sea to Mexico

Sea urchins
Echinoidea

Sea urchins are mainly nocturnal, and many species spend the day hidden in holes and crevices on the reef. Others, like diadem urchins, sometimes also rest in an open area, but crowded closely together in a large group for protection. Despite their largely defensive cluster of spines, sea urchins have predators, including various triggerfish, pufferfish and wrasses. Their nocturnal lifestyle is therefore regarded as a form of protective behaviour.

Grazing: Sea urchins feed primarily on minute algae, which they scrape off from rocks. Depending on species, some of them also eat, to some extent, a variety of non-mobile creatures, including coral polyps.

There are about 900 species worldwide. Many of them have spines that are sharp, and in the case of the diadem urchins, very long – more than 40 cm. Other species have very short or blunt spines. The slate pencil urchin, for example, has spines that are the thickness of a pencil and the length of a finger, but blunt. They use them to wedge themselves firmly in crevices at night.

Globe urchin
(Temnopleuridae)

Mespillia globulus

Size: 5 cm
Biology: The colour of the five broad bands without spines can vary from blue to green shades. Scrapes algae from hard surfaces. Camouflages itself with algae and fragments of coral and shell. More common at night, but not an unusual sight during the day out in the open.
Distribution: India, Maldives to Western Pacific

Hatpin urchin
(Diadematae)

Echinotrix calamaris

Size: 20 cm
Biology: The long spines are striped in juveniles (*see* photo), but in adults are usually black, very occasionally white. The spines can easily penetrate human skin and are very painful; 1–30 m.
Distribution: Red Sea to Hawaii and Pitcairn Islands

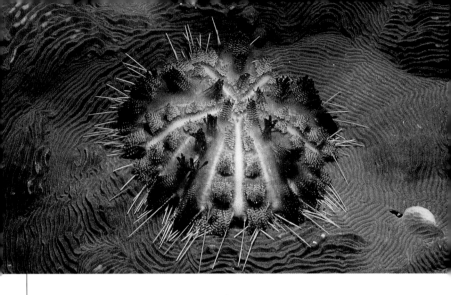

Fire urchin
Asthenosoma varium

Size: 28 cm
Biology: Usually hides during the day, tends to be active at night, out in the open. It often has commensal shrimps or prawns living on its surface. The spines can cause very painful injuries; 1–285 m.
Distribution: Oman to New Caledonia

Rousseau's urchin
Microcyphus rousseaui

Size: 5 cm
Biology: The areas without spines have a striking zigzag pattern. Scrapes algal growth and non-mobile animals from hard surfaces. A rare species, nocturnal; 1–30 m.
Distribution: Red Sea, Gulf of Oman to Southern Mozambique

Slate pencil urchin
Heterocentrotus mammillatus

Size: 30 cm
Biology: Has thick, blunt primary spines with a white ring at the base. Uses them to wedge itself into holes and crevices during the day. A nocturnal omnivore, often in shallow areas between 0.5–10 m.
Distribution: Red Sea to Polynesia

Flower urchin
Toxopneustes pileolus

Size: 15 cm
Biology: On coarse sand, coral debris and hard ground, covers itself with small stones and bits of coral and shell. Dangerous – the blossom-like prehensile claws can cause extremely painful poisonous injuries.
Distribution: East Africa to Cook Islands

Sea cucumbers
Holothuroidea

More than 1,200 species are known worldwide, from the polar regions to the tropics and from tidal zones to the deepest oceans. They range in size from 1 cm to more than 200 cm. On Indo-Pacific reefs, the large numbers of sea cucumbers on hard ground and sand are a familiar sight. Despite their appearance, sea cucumbers are echinoderms just like starfish, sea urchins, brittle stars and feather stars.

Debris feeder: Most of the sea cucumbers that live on reefs feed by swallowing large quantities of sand from the upper layers and utilizing the organic material (detritus) that it contains. Some species live mainly on hard surfaces, and pick up debris from the surface using the shield-like ends of their tentacles; this behaviour can often be seen by observing the leopard sea cucumber.

Yet other species have bushy tentacles and feed on plankton. They stretch their crown of tentacles out into open water in order to catch passing zooplankton and organic particles.

Some species release long, sticky and slightly poisonous threads if disturbed.

Weight watcher
Holothuria fuscogilva

Length: 50 cm
Biology: Sand and reefs. Feeds on debris and minute animals. A valued species in Asia, where it is known as the trepang.
Distribution: Red Sea to French Polynesia

Leopard sea cucumber
Pearsonothuria graeffei

Length: 50 cm
Biology: On rock and coral reefs; a good climber. Picks up debris using its flattened tentacles.
Distribution: Red Sea to French Polynesia

Sea apple
Pseudocolochirus violaceus

Length: 15 cm
Biology: Uses its bushy tentacles to catch plankton and detritus. Colours vary: yellow, blue and red. Frequently in groups.
Distribution: Indonesia to Philippines

Sea squirts
Ascidia

Amalgamation: There are solitary, social and colony-forming species of sea squirt. The social types live in small groups and are joined only at the base. Colony-forming species can be made up of many thousands of mini-individuals whose outer covering has amalgamated to form a single mass.

Pumping station: Sea squirts are small but high-performance pumps. They are active filter-feeders on organic particles and micro-organisms in the water around them. To feed, they pump large volumes of water through their bodies; some species that have been studied achieved a pump output of around 175 litres per day.

Fine-gauge filter: The water flows through a bronchial gut that makes up most of the inside of a sea squirt and acts as a filter bag. Even the most minute particles of 0.0005 mm are retained. The entire system is self-cleaning: at intervals, sea squirts draw themselves together and force water back out through the inlet openings. Any unwanted matter is ejected from the gullet, which is thus cleaned.

Blue tunicate
Rhopalaea crassa

Length: 6 cm
Biology: Blue to turquoise, sometimes with a translucent network pattern. Solitary, often in loose groups.
Distribution: Indonesia to Australia

Purple sea squirt
Polycarpa aurata

Length: 10 cm
Biology: Solitary, a common and widespread species. Only reproduces sexually. Closes its openings if disturbed.
Distribution: Sri Lanka to Micronesia

Robust sea squirt
Atriolum robustum

Length: 3 cm
Biology: Colony-forming: each of the small inlet openings represents one individual, and they all share one large outlet opening.
Distribution: Indonesia to Western Pacific

Index

Ablabys taenianotus **52**
Abudefduf vaigiensis **98**
Acanthaster planci **208**
Acanthopagrus bifasciatus **83**
Acanthuridae **130**
Acanthurus leucosternon **130**
   mata **130**
   sohal **130**
   triostegus **132**
Acropora clathrata **178**
   formosa **181**
Actinaria **176**
Aeoliscus strigatus **43**
Aetobatus narinari **18**
Alcyonaria **166**
Aluterus scriptus **140**
Amblyeleotris aurora **122**
Amblyglyphidodon aureus **98**
Amphiprion clarkii **100**
   melanopus **103**
   nigripes **102**
   ocellaris **100**
   perideraion **102**
Amphiprioninae **100**
Amplexidiscus fenestrafer **175**
anemone, adhesive **176**
   giant tube **174**
   magnificent **176**
anemone fish, Clark's **100**
   false clown **100**
   Maldives **102**
   pink **102**
   spinecheek **103**
angelfish, Arabian **94**
   blue-girdled **96**
   emperor **94**
   regal **96**
   threespot **97**
   zebra lyretail **97**
Annella mollis **170**
Antennariidae **30**
Antennarius commersoni **30**
   pictus **30**
anthias, Red Sea **62**
   scalefin **62**
Anthiinae **62**
Antipathes dichotoma **182**
Antipathidae **182**
Apogon aureus **70**
Apogonidae **70**
Apolemichthys trimaculatus **97**
Arothron diadematus **148**
   mappa **146**
   nigropunctatus **148**
   stellatus **146**
Ascidia **216**
Asteroidea **208**
Asthenosoma varium **212**
Atriolum robustum **216**
Aulostomidae **35**
Aulostomus chinensis **35**
Aurelia aurita **164**

Balistapus undulatus **136**
Balistidae **136**
Balistoides conspicillum **139**
   viridescens **138**
balloonfish **150**
bannerfish, schooling **93**
barracuda, great **135**
Batoidei **18**
Belonidae **36**
bigeye, crescent-tail **61**
Bivalvia **196**
Blenniidae **116**
blenny, Midas **116**
   Red Sea mimic **116**
Bolbometapon muricatum **108**
boxfish, solor **144**
   spotted **144**
   yellow **142**
bream, bridled monocle **82**
   humpnose big-eye **80**
   striped large-eye **80**
bristleworm, peacock **184**
brittle star, long-spined **207**
Bryaninops natans **123**
   youngei **123**
burrfish, orbicular **150**
butterflyfish, Bennett's **91**
   longnose **93**
   masked **92**
   melon **91**
   red-back **92**
   scrawled **90**
   spotted **88**
   threadfin **90**
   white collar **88**

Caesionidae **76**
Caesio suevica **76**
   xanthonota **76**
Callechelys marmorata **26**
Callionymidae **118**
Calloplesiops altivelis **59**
Calpurnus verrucosus **190**
Canthigaster papua **149**
   valentini **149**
Carangidae **72**
Carangoides bajad **72**
Caranx ignobilis **72**
Carcharhinidae **16**

Carcharhinus amblyrhynchos
  16
  melanopterus **16**
cardinalfish, five-lined **70**
  fing-tailed **70**
  tiger **70**
Carpilius convexus **204**
Cassiopea andromeda **164**
catfish, striped eel **28**
Centriscidae **43**
Cephalopholis miniata **64**
  sexmaculata **64**
Cephea cephea **164**
Ceriantharia **174**
Cerianthus cf. *filiformis* **174**
Cetoscarus bicolor **111**
Chaetodon auriga **90**
  bennetti **91**
  collare **88**
  guttatissimus **88**
  meyeri **90**
  paucifasciatus **92**
  semilarvatus **92**
  trifasciatus **91**
Chaetodontidae **88**
Charonia tritonis **190**
Cheilinus lunulatus **104**
  undulatus **104**
Cheilodipterus macrodon **70**
  quinquelineatus **70**
Chelonia mydas **154**
Chloea flava **184**
Chlororus sordidus **110**
Choriaster granulatus **208**
Choridactylinae **51**
chromis, green **98**
Chromis viridis **98**
chromodoris, Kune's **194**
Chromodoris kuniei **194**
  quadricolor **192**

Cirrhipathes anguina **182**
  spiralis **182**
Cirrhitidae **68**
clam digger **202**
clam, squamose giant **196**
clownfish, cinnamon **103**
Comanthina schlegelii **206**
comet **59**
Conus textile **190**
coral, brain **181**
  branching black **182**
  bubble **180**
  common toadstool **168**
  finger leather **169**
  Klunzinger's soft **166**
  lobate leather **168**
  maze **180**
  net fire **162**
  spiral **182**
  staghorn **181**
  table **178**
  vibrant soft **166**
  yellow scroll **178**
corallimorph, balloon **175**
Corallimorpharia **175**
cornetfish **34**
Corythoichthys flavofasciatus
  42
cowfish, longhorn **145**
  thornback **145**
crab, anemone hermit **203**
  harlequin **204**
  porcelain anemone **203**
  red reef **204**
Crinoidea **206**
Crustacea **200**
Cryptodendron adhaesivum
  176
cucumber, leopard sea **214**
cuttlefish, pharaoh **199**

Cyclichthys orbicularis **150**

Dactyloptena orientalis **54**
Dactylopteridae **54**
Dactylopus dactylopus **118**
damselfish, golden **98**
Dardanus pedunculatus **203**
dartfish, fire **125**
Dasyatis kuhlii **20**
Delphinidae **157**
Dendrochirus biocellatus **47**
  brachypterus **46**
  zebra **47**
Dendronephthya hemprichi
  166
  klunzingeri **166**
devilfish, spiny **51**
Diadematae **210**
Diodon holocanthus **150**
  hystrix **150**
Diodontidae **150**
dolphin, Indo-Pacific
  bottlenose **157**
dottyback, sunrise **60**
dragonet, fingered **118**
dragonfish, little **37**
dugong **156**
Dugong dugon **156**

Echeneidae **57**
Echeneis naucrates **57**
Echinoidea **210**
Echinotrix calamaris **210**
eel, marbled snake **26**
  Napoleon snake **26**
Elapidae **155**
Ellisella juncea **170**
emperor, yellowfin **80**
Ephippidae **126**
Epibulus insidiator **107**

Epinephelus fasciatus **64**
  malabaricus **66**
  tukula **67**
Escenius gravieri **116**
  midas **116**
Eurypegasus draconis **37**

fangblenny, bluestriped **116**
fan, giant sea **170**
  knotted **170**
feather, common sea **172**
feather star, variable bushy **206**
filefish, blacksaddle **140**
  harlequin **140**
  scrawled **140**
fish, Mandarin **118**
  spot-fin porcupine **150**
Fistularia commersonii **34**
Fistulariidae **34**
flathead, tentacled **53**
flatworm, Bedford's **189**
  divided **188**
  fuchsia **188**
  glorious **186**
  gold-dotted **186**
  Orsak's **189**
Forcipiger flavissimus **93**
frogfish, giant **30**
  painted **30**
fusilier, bluestreak **76**
  Red Sea **76**
  yellowback **76**

Genicanthus caudovittatus **97**
Gnathanodon speciosus **72**
Gnathodentex aurolineatus **80**
goatfish, manybar **86**

Red Sea **86**
  yellowfin **86**
Gobiidae **120**
Gobiodon citrinus **120**
goby, aurora **122**
  citron **120**
  gold-headed sleeper **120**
  orange-dash **122**
  pink-eye **123**
  signal **120**
  whipcoral **123**
Gorgonacea **170**
Grammistes sexlineatus **58**
Grammistinae **58**
grouper, blacktip **64**
  coral **64**
  Malabar **66**
  potato **67**
  roving coral **66**
  saddle **64**
gurnard, Oriental flying **54**
Gymnosarda unicolor **114**
Gymnothorax breedeni **24**
  favagineus **22**
  fimbriatus **22**
  griseus **25**
  javanicus **22**
  meleagris **24**

Haemulidae **78**
Halichoeres hortulanus **107**
hawkfish, arc-eye **68**
  freckled **68**
  longnose **68**
Helcogramma striatum **115**
Heniochus diphreutes **93**
Heteractis magnifica **176**
Heterocentrotus mammillatus **213**
Heteroxenia fuscescens **169**

Hexabranchus sanguineus **194**
Hippocampus bargibanti **40**
  taeniopterus **40**
Hipposcarus harid **111**
Holocentridae **32**
Holothuria fuscogilva **214**
Holothuroidea **214**
houndfish, crocodile **36**
hydroid, stinging **163**
Hymenocera elegans **200**

idol, Moorish **134**
Inimicus didactylus **51**
invertebrates **159**

jawfish, gold-specs **124**
jellyfish, common **164**
  crown **164**
  moon **164**
  upside-down **164**

krait, black & white sea **155**

Labridae **104**
Lactoria cornuta **145**
  fornasini **145**
Laticauda colubrina **155**
Lethrinidae **80**
Lethrinus erythracanthus **80**
Linckia laevigata **208**
lionfish, common **44**
  Mombassa **46**
  shortfin **46**
  spotfin **44**
  twinspot **47**
  zebra **47**
Lissocarcinus orbicularis **204**

lizardfish, two-spot **29**
Lobophytum sp. **168**
lobster, painted spiny **202**
Lutjanidae **74**
Lutjanus gibbus **74**
    kasmira **74**
lyretail, yellow-edged **67**

Macolor macularis **74**
Macrorhynchia philippina
    163
Maiazoon orsaki **189**
Malacanthidae **56**
Malacanthus brevirostris **56**
mammals **153**
manta **18**
Manta birostris **18**
Melithaea ochracea **170**
Mespillia globulus **210**
Microcyphus rousseaui **212**
Millepora dichotoma **162**
Milleporidae **162**
Monacanthidae **140**
Monodactylidae **85**
Monodactylus argenteus
    85
Monotaxis grandoculis **80**
moonfish, silver **85**
moray, blackcheek **24**
    fimbriated **22**
    geometric **25**
    giant **22**
    honeycomb **22**
    ribbon **25**
    whitemouth **24**
Mullidae **86**
Mulloidichthys vanicolensis
    86
Muraenidae **22**
Myripristis vittata **32**

Naso hexacanthus **133**
    vlamingii **133**
Nebrius ferrugineus **14**
Negombata corticata **160**
Nemateleotris magnifica **125**
Nembrotha purpureolineolata
    192
Nemipteridae **82**
Neoniphon sammara **32**
Neopetrolisthes oshima **203**
nudibranch, eyespot **195**
    purple **192**
    pyjama **192**
    Tryon's **192**
Nudibranchia **192**

Octopodidae **198**
Octopus cyanea **198**
octopus, day **198**
Odontodactylus scyllarus
    205
Odonus niger **136**
Ophichthidae **26**
Ophichthys bonaparti **26**
Ophiotrix savignyi **207**
Ophiuroidea **207**
Opistognathidae **124**
Opistognathus randalli **124**
Orectolobiformes **14**
Ostraciidae **142**
Ostracion cubicus **142**
    meleagris **144**
    solorensis **144**
ovula, umbilical **190**
Oxycheilinus diagrammus
    106
Oxycirrhites typus **68**
Oxymonacanthus halli **140**
oyster, orange-mouth
    thorny **196**

Pachyseris speciosa **180**
Panulirus versicolor **202**
Papilloculiceps longiceps **53**
Paracirrhites arcatus **68**
    forsteri **68**
Paraluteres prionurus **140**
Parapercis hexophthalma
    112
Parapriacanthus ransonneti
    84
parrotfish, bicolour **111**
    bullethead **110**
    humphead **108**
    longnose **111**
    roundhead **108**
    rusty **110**
Parupeneus forsskali **86**
    multifasciatus **86**
Pearsonothuria graeffei **214**
Pegasidae **37**
Pempheridae **84**
Pennatulacea **172**
Phyllidia ocellata **195**
Pinguipidae **112**
pipefish, network **42**
    ornate ghost **38**
    robust ghost **38**
Plagiotremus rhinorhynchus
    116
Platax orbicularis **126**
    teira **126**
Platyhelminthes **186**
Platycephalidae **53**
Platygyra daedalea **181**
Plectorhinchus albovittatus
    78
    chaetodonoides **78**
    vittatus **78**
Plectropomus pessuliferus
    66

Plerogyra sinuosa **180**
Plesiopidae **59**
Plotosidae **28**
Plotosus lineatus **28**
Plumulariidae **163**
Polycarpa aurata **216**
Polychaeta **184**
polyp, button **173**
Pomacanthidae **94**
Pomacanthus imperator **94**
  maculosus **94**
  narvachus **96**
Pomacentridae **98**
Porifera **160**
Premnas biaculeatus **103**
Priacanthidae **61**
Priacanthus hamrur **61**
Prosobranchia **190**
Protopalythoa sp. **173**
Pseudanthias squamipinnis
  62
  taeniatus **62**
Pseudobalistes
  flavimarginatus **139**
  fuscus **138**
Pseudobiceros bedfordi **189**
  gloriosus **186**
Pseudoceros cf. *ferugineus*
  188
  dimidiatus **188**
Pseudochromidae **60**
Pseudochromis flavivertex
  60
Pseudocolochirus violaceus
  214
Pseudosquilla ciliata **205**
pteraeolidia, serpent **195**
Pteraeolidia ianthina **195**
Ptereleotridae **125**
Pterocaesio tile **76**

Pteroides sp. **172**
Pteroinae **44**
Pterois antennata **44**
  mombasae **46**
  volitans **44**
puffer, blackspotted **148**
  map **146**
  masked **148**
  star **146**
  Valentin's sharpnose
    149
Pygoplites diacanthus **96**

rabbitfish, golden **128**
  gold-spotted **128**
  two-barred **128**
ray, porcupine **18**
  spotted eagle **18**
razorfish, coral **43**
reptiles **153**
Rhincodon typus **14**
Rhinecanthus assasi **136**
Rhinomuraena quaesita **25**
Rhopalaea crassa **216**
Risbecia tryoni **192**

sand-diver, Red Sea **113**
sandperch, speckled **112**
Sarcophyton trocheliophorum
  168
Sargocentron spiniferum **32**
Scaridae **108**
Scarus ferrugineus **110**
  strongylocephalus **108**
Scleractinia **178**
Scolopsis bilineatus **82**
Scombridae **114**
Scorpaenidae **48**
Scorpaenopsis diabolus **48**
  oxycephala **48**

scorpionfish, devil **48**
  leaf **48**
  tasselled **48**
Scyphozoa **164**
Scyllarides tridacnophaga
  202
sea apple **214**
seabream, twobar **83**
seahorse, common **40**
  pygmy **40**
sea squirt, purple **216**
  robust **216**
sea star, granulated **208**
Sepia pharaonis **199**
Sepiidae **199**
sergeant, Indo-Pacific **98**
Serranidae **64**
shark, blacktip reef **16**
  grey reef **16**
  leopard **14**
  tawny nurse **14**
  whale **14**
  whitetip reef **16**
sharksucker **57**
shell, textile cone **190**
shrimp, banded coral **200**
  common mantis **205**
  harlequin **200**
  peacock mantis **205**
Siganidae **128**
Siganus guttatus **128**
  stellatus **128**
  virgatus **128**
Signigobius biocellatus **120**
Sinularia leptoclados **169**
snapper, bluestripe **74**
  humpback **74**
  midnight **74**
soapfish, sixline **58**
soldierfish, white-tip **32**

Solenostomidae **38**
Solenostomus cyanopterus
    38
  paradoxus **38**
spadefish, circular **126**
  longfin **126**
Spanish dancer **194**
Sparidae **83**
Sphyraena barracuda **135**
Sphyraenidae **135**
Spirobranchus giganteus **184**
Spondylus varius **196**
sponge, barrel **160**
  Red Sea **160**
squirrelfish, sabre **32**
  spotfin **32**
star, blue **208**
starfish, crown-of-thorns
    208
stargazer, whitemargin **55**
Stegostoma fasciatum **14**
Stenopus hispidus **200**
stingray, black-spotted **20**
  blue-spotted **21**
  Kuhl's **20**
stonefish, reef **50**
surgeonfish, convict **132**
  powderblue **130**
  Sohal **130**
  yellowmask **130**
sweeper, glassy **84**
sweetlips, giant **78**
  many-spotted **78**
  Oriental **78**
Synanceia verrucosa **50**
Synanceinae **50**
Synchiropus splendidus **118**
Syngnathidae **40, 42**
Synodontidae **29**

Synodus binotatus **29**

Taenionatus triacanthus **48**
Taeniura lymma **21**
  meyeni **20**
tang, yellowtail **132**
Temnopleuridae **210**
Testudines **154**
Tetraodontidae **146**
Tetrarogidae **52**
Thalassoma hardwicke **106**
Thysanozoon nigropapillosum
    186
tilefish, flagtail **56**
toby, Papuan **149**
torpedo, leopard **21**
Torpedo panthera **21**
Toxopneustes pileolus **213**
trevally, giant **72**
  golden **72**
  orange-spotted **72**
Triaenodon obesus **16**
Trichonotidae **113**
Trichonotus nikei **113**
Tridacna squamosa **196**
triggerfish, clown **139**
  orange-lined **136**
  Picasso **136**
  redtoothed **136**
  Titan **138**
  yellow-margin **139**
  yellow-spotted **138**
triplefin, striped **115**
Tripterygiidae **115**
trumpetfish **35**
trumpet, Triton's **190**
tuna, dogtooth **114**
tunicate, blue **216**
Turbinaria mesenterina **178**

Tursiops aduncus **157**
turtle, green sea **154**
Tylosurus crocodilus **36**

unicornfish, bignose **133**
  sleek **133**
Uranoscopidae **55**
Uranoscopus sulphureus **55**
urchin, fire **212**
  flower **213**
  globe **210**
  hatpin **210**
  Rousseau's **212**
  slate pencil **213**
Urogymnus asperrimus **18**

Valenciennea strigata **120**
  puellaris **122**
Variola louti **67**

waspfish, cockatoo **52**
weight watcher **214**
whip, red cluster **170**
worm, christmas tree **184**
wrasse, bandcheek **106**
  broomtail **104**
  checkerboard **107**
  humphead **104**
  sixbar **106**
  slingjaw **107**

xenid, pulsating **169**
Xestospongia testudinaria
    160

Zanclidae **134**
Zanclus cornutus **134**
Zebrasoma xanthurum **132**
Zoantharia **173**

First published in the United Kingdom in 2011 by John Beaufoy Publishing Limited,
11 Blenheim Court, 316 Woodstock Road, Oxford OX2 7NS, England
www.johnbeaufoy.com

10 9 8 7 6 5 4 3 2 1

The information given in this book has been carefully researched and checked, but
the publishers cannot accept any liability. The planning and carrying out of dives are
the sole responsibility of divers themselves. There is no warranty on the part of the
authors, publishers or any persons commissioned by them.

ISBN 978-1-906780-55-5

Editor of German edition: Monika Weymann
Cover design and original layout and typesetting: Populärgrafik, Stuttgart
Translation for English edition: Interlinguæ Srl, Parma, Italy

With 295 photographs by the authors.

Cover photo of a raccoon butterfly fish by Manuela Kirschner

Back cover photos, l. to r.:
Giant frogfish, Emperor angelfish, Striped triplefin

English edition typeset by D & N Publishing, Baydon, Wiltshire

Printed and bound in Malaysia by Times Offset (M) Sdn. Bhd.